John Newell was born in Brisbane ... Education Degree majoring in ... University of Tasmania. Since ag... ... numerous choirs, chamber ensembles, musical theatr... ...ductions, and barbershop harmony groups. He sang the Lead part in *Realtime* when it won the 2005 International Barbershop Quartet Championship, after earlier winning two Australian championships as the Lead of *Southern Cross* quartet. John now lives in Canada with his wife and three children. He is a professional vocal performance coach of individual singers and ensembles.

John Newell

LET IT OUT

Train your voice to be free.
Free your voice to be trained.

ISBN 978-0-9920078-0-5 (paperback)

ISBN 978-0-9920078-1-2 (electronic edition)

Front cover design by Oliver Merrill.

www.letitoutvocals.com

www.facebook.com/letitoutvocals

Let It Out is also available in electronic format for Kindle, Kobo and other electronic devices.

You can purchase electronic versions through:

www.amazon.com

(as well as all Amazon websites worldwide)

www.kobo.com

and the Google Play Store

play.google.com

To Corinne

I realize very well that the reader has no great need to know all this; but I need to tell him.

Rousseau, *Les Confessions.*

We are what we repeatedly do. Excellence, then, is not an act, but a habit.

Aristotle.

Obsessions are what we have instead of normality.

Clive James, *May Week Was In June*, 1990.

Acknowledgments

To all I have sung with and for over the years, I owe enormous gratitude for sharing the journey with me.

To all people who have attempted to coach me – some successfully – I offer my thanks and admiration for your patience. I have learned from every one of you.

To Sandy Marron, thank you for being there at the right time to open the door to this journey of discovery.

To those whom I have coached, thank you for your trust and your friendship.

I had written more than half of this book before I came across and read Lilli Lehmann's book, *My Singing Art* (*Meine Gesangkunst*), first published in 1902. I was surprised and gratified by the many similarities of our approaches. I arrived independently at many ideas expressed in this my book after years of experience, coaching, practice and thinking, yet I offer profound gratitude and tribute to Lilli. Her work has further strengthened, emboldened, embellished and inspired my beliefs. I urge any and all singers to read her most excellent writings.

Foreword

by Graeme Morton AM

We all know someone who says that they cannot sing. Engage with them for a while and you may well find that this is a knowledge that has been given to them by another, possibly a teacher or conductor at school. There seem to be many children who were cruelly told, typically by school teachers, that they could not sing.

Yet singing is as natural an activity as talking or breathing itself. In a child's development it may well be one of the first creative or expressive acts. It is core to who we are as human beings. When we see a child (or an adult) casually singing as they perform some unrelated task, it seems to me that we are observing the brain at play – pleasing itself spontaneously and often thoughtlessly. Many music teachers now have accepted responsibility for the education of every student, and when they see a child who cannot sing, acknowledge that they can help their student find their voice. And so we come to the motto that many teachers adopt in encouraging reluctant students – "if you can speak, you can sing". And, of course, it is true.

Yet singing is also an art. Our desire as humans to formalize, to develop, and to categorize, aligns with our desire to perform, to project the self to others, and to share. Some people overact to the formality of the artform that we have created and attack the task with determination. While mental determination is important, it often spills over into physical determination. This is not so good.

Singing is first and foremost a muscular activity. Muscles grow and develop with training, and therefore voices can be developed. Further, we now know so much more about the processes of singing. Only recently have we been able to *see* the singing voice at work. The operation of every other musical instrument has always been clearly observable, but the voice, until relatively recent advances in technology, could be understood only hypothetically.

But what of innate ability ("Oh you have such a gift for music, I wish I was born with your talents.")? Well the jury is still out on that question. We can confidently say, based on recent research into expertise, that the notion that musical giftedness is genetically acquired is now seen as far less significant than in the past. This research on the development of expertise has changed the perception of giftedness to a significant degree.

Ericsson and others have demonstrated that the amount of time spent in deliberate practice determines success more than talent alone. Just what is *deliberate practice?* Whatever it is, it cannot avoid self-reflection, self-assessment, and constant evaluation. This is where this book comes to the fore. *Let It Out* encourages the kind of deliberate practice that will help you grow as a singer.

It is the 'deliberate' in deliberate practice that is important. Watch out. Practice does not (necessarily) make perfect. It may mean that you have just done lots of practice. The aim of musicians, for whom practice is of course a *sine qua non*, is to gain expertise as well as experience. Therefore our practice needs to be informed, in order to be deliberate. Otherwise you may only be what researchers refer to as an 'experienced non-expert'.

John Newell's excellent book invites such an informed, reflective stance. It is in this role of the singer as self-assessor that *Let It Out* becomes a valuable resource for singers and teachers of singing. It encourages reflection and self-awareness. It is jam-packed with practical tips and sound advice. It is clear and concise. In some senses it is 'everything you wanted to know about singing but were afraid to ask'. But more than that, this book is encouraging. There are many books on singing that I read because I feel almost obligated. This volume, I can assure you, is not one of those. In our busy lives it need not even be read sequentially. Keep the book nearby, and open it up randomly – it still makes good sense and allows you to confirm or reconsider your perceptions of the singing process. It is a resource you can return to often.

This book is written by one who can do, who has done, and who teaches. Rather than tell singers *what* to do, it allows us to reflect on *how* to do. It reminds us that to sing is an art, yet one that must remain simple and grounded in the roots of physical ease. John Newell took himself from singing Barbershop in Hobart, Australia, geographically close to the bottom of the world, to the top of the competition world that was winning the International Quartet Championship.

How did he get there? You may not find the answer to that in this book, although you will find a great deal about what he learned along the way. But how might **you** get there, to wherever you dream your singing might take you? Open up *Let It Out* and start reading – it will help you find out!

Graeme Morton.

Choral Fellow, University of Queensland Conservatorium of Music, Australia.
Director of Music, St John's Cathedral, Brisbane.
Director, Brisbane Chamber Choir.
Member, Order of Australia.

Contents

Introduction

Every singer needs help sometimes, even the best ones. But *how* do we sing better?

I am convinced that a singer's pathway to improvement begins in the mind. Many singers focus on the physical side, which is indeed crucial, but volumes have been published about the physiological side of singing, by people far better qualified than I. My intention is not to rediscover the road that has been well travelled already, nor to reinvent the wheel.

This book is intended as a handbook or guide for singers. It is about opening a singer's mind and body to pathways that he/she may not have considered. I have seen singers become hung up on certain approaches, techniques and mindsets that they believe are helpful but in fact cause only moderate improvement and sometimes stagnation. I have done this myself, many times. For years, I, and other singers I knew, persisted with the same approaches that had been drummed in by teachers, even though that persistence resulted in little to no progress for a period of years. A fixed mindset hindered my progress. I had always been a competent and solid singer, passionate also, but once my mind and body were opened, my singing improved rapidly. I also became more driven. Once I spent time reflecting on how it happened, and how it fit into my philosophy and persona as a performer and teacher, I realized I could help others.

My approach revolves around the idea that coaching should *reveal* a singer's best vocal production. Instead of building or creating, I believe a singer's best voice is already built and needs merely to be released, enhanced and refined. Revealing *your* best singing is about releasing certain habits, releasing your mind, and releasing your body, so your soul can be released through your voice.

After all, singing is an art. As my compatriot Clive James wrote in his 1990 book *May Week Was In June*, 'works of art can be inspired only by individual passion'. It requires more than technique. Many of us can become engrossed in learning to sing with better technique, often obsessively. Yet all the exercises, scales and repetitions in the world will not make a better artist, unless that artist knows that the technique fits inside the art, instead of vice versa.

When I was twenty-five, I thought I knew a lot about singing. I didn't. Through my early years, I always had ability on stage and had been told by stage directors that I had a strong presence and good voice. But I barely understood what was required to go further, if I understood at all. It wasn't until I reached my thirties that I began to understand how my voice worked and how to use it more effectively and efficiently. It was only then that something I had long known finally became clear – that a singer's journey of improvement and discovery is lifelong. Perhaps at some things I am a slow learner. Perhaps I am a late bloomer. Perhaps for years I allowed my ego to close my mind and convince me that my technique was already excellent. Perhaps I thought I had always done well on my abilities alone and didn't need a lot of instruction to enhance them. Perhaps I had clutched onto some small points taught to me by others and clung too tightly, believing those points mapped the pathway to perfection. Perhaps I thought the right people and the right opportunities would keep coming my way without any effort from me. Perhaps I hoped I would be discovered and be set for life. Perhaps I was too aggressive about some things I wanted.

When I was thirty-five, after twenty-nine years of singing – eighteen of them singing barbershop music – and after moving from Australia to Canada, I was fortunate enough to be in *Realtime*, a quartet that won the 2005 International Barbershop Quartet Contest. Originally I had been attracted to barbershop because it combined all the things I loved and relished – individual singing skill, ensemble singing skill, challenging music, theatrical stage performance, emotional commitment, artistic risk-taking, meticulous preparation, continuous reinvention, attention to detail, camaraderie, audience rapport, and so on. Winning the International Championship was a huge moment in a long journey and something that very few singers have achieved. All four of us in *Realtime* were fortunate enough to be part of a special combination of voices. We were fortunate enough to be at similar stages of life and headed in similar directions. We were fortunate enough to be on a similar journey of discovery together. Special combinations come along very rarely.

It became clear to me that I had learned to follow my heart. This is what all artists do, not just in their work but in their lives. Three years before *Realtime*'s win, I moved overseas with no agenda other than to explore a new life with a wonderful woman, who is now my wife and the mother of our three beautiful children. By being honest, passionate and committed about the one thing that was most important to me, other opportunities opened. I became open to change. They opened further when I took steps to explore that change. The opportunities came along because I had visualized them and desired them for years, and then I released them from my consciousness when I understood my personal priorities.

Why?

First, I worked out what I valued most. I made that my prime focus with my heart and soul. Second, while performing was my passion, it had been put in proper perspective, leaving me free to explore it from a new perspective and in a new life. It was important that it remain a passion and not become an obsession. Third, sorting out my priorities created the conditions for new opportunities.

Once I knew 'who I was', I was in an ideal state to open my mind and learn a different approach to singing. I learned that the physical process of singing should be easy, which contrasted with the very muscular approach I had been taught, and had used, previously. I saw and experienced the importance of free, open, and relaxed vocal production. Tension became my enemy. I learned that tension not only reduces the resonance of the voice, it blocks the true expression of a performer's soul. A free and relaxed delivery enables a free expression. The harder I tried, the less effective I was. The more I gave up control, the better my singing was, and the more powerful was the truth in my performance.

Once I understood my identity as a performer, including my strengths and weaknesses, I was free to envision a performance before I even started learning the music. I have noticed many singers work in reverse – they start with the notes and words, learn them, and then consider how to present the material. I had been getting things backwards all those years. Before learning the material and preparing the technical process needed to deliver it, I had to know what I was truly expressing. Right from the start I needed a vision for the music. The big picture had to come first. The more specific I made that big picture, the more specific I was able to be with the smaller details. For me, the art inspired and guided the technique. Not vice versa. The passion inspired and guided the preparation. Not vice versa.

Now I approach any new performance idea from this viewpoint. If the song or piece or role inspires me and I quickly develop a vision for it, I do it. If it does not 'speak' to me, I don't do it.

I am not a perfect singer and am comfortable knowing that I never will be. There is no such thing as a perfect singer, nor a perfect performance. This is a liberating concept because instead of pursuing unattainable perfection I now pursue truth and soul in a performance, while always aiming for my highest standards.

My journey of singing and performing is continuous. My learning is continuous. The increase in my awareness is continuous.

I hope the same for you.

Note:

While I do not claim to be the world's greatest singer, I am proud of my achievements. Winning an International Quartet Championship is more difficult than most singers know and has been achieved by so few. I will always be astonished and honoured to be part of that small group.

In addition, I grew up including the 'u' in words like 'honour',' favour' and 'labour', while also spelling the noun as 'practice' and the verb as 'practise'. If these are foreign to you, please bear with my ingrained habits.

Guidelines, Disclaimers & Provisos

This book will not make you a star or an expert. No book can do that. Only you can.

This book does not take the place of a good voice teacher. Far from it.

Use this book as a guide when singing and performing exercises. It is a checklist, if you like, or a handbook. The exercises outlined herein do not constitute the complete list of exercises that you will ever need. Far from it. There are thousands of helpful exercises. You and I can find them at will in books and on the internet. By all means use them. I am not here to repeat the work of others, but to demonstrate fundamentals that should apply when doing exercises and to provide exercises that support those fundamentals. As far as I am concerned, *how* you do an exercise is equally important as the exercise itself. I do not believe in asking a student to perform scales and arpeggios and other such exercises until that student knows *how* and *why* they should be done. Otherwise, repetition of exercises can and will reinforce old and bad habits. ***First set your voice free, then perform a variety of exercises using that free voice.*** Create appropriate habits and apply those in everything you vocalize.

This book is intended as a platform to help you on a new, and lifelong, journey of discovery and awareness. It is not an exhaustive resource or comprehensive 'bible' of singing. No book can be. As in golf, a book about how to play cannot substitute for proper coaching, practice and play. However, it can serve as a foundation or point of reference for when you have issues and questions.

This is my attempt to demystify singing.

Sometimes the most fundamental principles can provide the solution to a problem. Over-analyzing and searching for new techniques can complicate matters and take you away from your centre.

Many experts have published excellent materials explaining the physiological actions of breathing and singing. They have done so far more exhaustively and learnedly than I ever can. Instead of covering ground that has been well covered already, I offer some approaches and techniques that I have found successful for me as well as for singers and ensembles I have coached.

There is no one true method for singing that will suit every singer. This book provides a variety of ideas and approaches for you to try. It is vital that you (1) experiment with everything your voice can do, (2) have a trusted person or coach listen to you and provide feedback, and (3) listen to your body so everything you sing always feels effortless, unmuscled, free and consistent. Any sensation of muscle tension or tightness or fatigue, in any part of your body, should be regarded as a warning.

There is no single technique or exercise that solves all problems. Becoming a better singer is a journey of discovery, as well as some trial and error.

Not everyone can be a superstar. However, everyone can always strive for a new personal best.

Like actors, there are many singers who are not as successful as they want to be. Many are unemployed or under-employed. True artists love what they do and do what they love. But they must be practical, as must you and I. Pursue your dreams while also recognizing your limitations. Not everyone has the ability or connections or fortunate events to become a star. Even if you must work day after day at a job you hate, just to pay the bills, you can still love your singing and do it with your entire soul.

Step out of your accustomed 'comfort zone' and open your mind. Inflexible opinions are dangerous for any performer. They are equally dangerous for a coach.

Clear your mind and expectations. Prepare for a journey that never ends. There is always something to improve. There is always something to learn. There is always a different way of going about something.

Chapter 1

Why 'Let It Out'?

Your natural voice is your best voice. The voice that simply falls out of you with minimum physical effort and maximum physical freedom is loaded with resonance and is the foundation of all your singing. It connects to your emotions and your soul. Simply allow your voice to spill out. Excessive effort and muscled technique can disconnect you from your natural voice. Get yourself out of the way.

Let it out.

Learning to release your true, natural voice, and doing it consistently, will leave you ideally placed to receive training in a variety of singing styles. You will have a foundation for those other genres, along with greater flexibility to adapt to other training. By mastering the natural voice, you will find that adapting to other genres requires only subtle adjustments instead of major actions. I urge all singers to discover and master this natural approach before embarking on training for specialized vocal styles.

Let it out.

Your voice is yours alone. No one else has it. Attempting to sound like your idol rarely leads to long-term success, if ever. Learn from other singers you admire, be inspired by them, but do not copy them. They achieved their best by learning how to use their own unique voices, not by imitating others. You must learn how to sound like *you*. Remove unnecessary actions and thoughts – such as trying to sing like someone else – and release your voice freely. Because of habitual muscle and thought patterns, it may suddenly feel like your singing is 'out of control'. But that is freedom. With that freedom, your voice can connect properly to your true emotions. Release your natural voice and your soul together through music.

Let it out.

A sculptor selected a large chunk of marble and began chipping and carving. In time, the sculpture was finished. People told him he had created a beautiful statue. The sculptor said he *created* nothing. The statue was always there. He had merely cleared away the outer pieces.

Many singers should do the same. Remove unnecessary muscle habits and complicated thought patterns so you can reveal the true, natural voice that is already there within you. So many singers do not know what they have within them, due to restrictive habits and thoughts.

Let it out.

The most successful singers do not just play by the rules and wait for success. They change the game by doing it their own way. Innovators and ground-breakers did not do so for the sake of it; they simply declared who they really were. If you want to increase your success, do it your way.

Let it out.

Relaxing vocal production to achieve optimum resonance with minimal effort can be one of the hardest things for a singer to learn. The journey is long and transformational, but well worth it.

Let it out.

There is something special and unique about your singing. Find what it is.

Let it out.

Be yourself. Do not pretend. Do not perform. Be your true self.

Be.

Let it out.

The artistry and passion pre-empt the technique. Not vice versa.

Let it out.

Singing is art. It is about expressing what you think and feel. It is not about pursuing glory. Chasing rewards for their own sake rarely results in success and can be an empty, unfulfilling process. Rewards come from pursuing your passion and being true to yourself. Do it because you love it and let the rewards come from that. The rewards may not appear in the form you expect.

Let it out.

Chapter 2

It's All Mental

Have you reached a plateau in your singing? Do you keep banging your head against a glass ceiling? Do you always follow the same processes? If you do what you have always done, you get what you have always got.

The key to improvement as a singer is to open your mind and change your mental patterns. Freeing your mental processes will help free your voice and body.

Some singers appear to labour under the impression that repeating specific physical exercises will produce improvement. To an extent this is true. However, if it were wholly true then sheer physical repetition would produce the world's best singers. Truly important are the *habits* a singer forms. Some appear to get stuck on one way of doing things, either because they know no other way or because their minds have been convinced that that one way is 'correct'.

It is not enough for you simply to repeat exercises like you are building muscle and fitness for a physical purpose. That focuses on *what* to do. What about *how* and *why* you do it? This is the mental side of things and the how and the why have profound effect on the what. Your mental set up dictates your physical set up and action. Mental release is essential for providing muscle release and for changing muscle memory.

For example, consider breathing. Continuous repetition of breathing exercises can produce improved efficiency and strength. However, without considering how or why you are doing the exercises, that repetition can also cause some physical habits that are unhelpful to your singing. How you think when preparing to breathe has a strong bearing not only on your breathing, but also your physical stance and freedom. How you breathe and how you release tension are not only physical actions, they are mental actions also.

The first step toward improving your singing is always mental. You must open your mind in order to see a pathway you may never have noticed or considered before. The next several steps are mental, also, as you explore, test, and trust the new pathway. The physical and physiological aspects will follow where your mind goes. So, choose a pathway that is fresh, new, and uncluttered.

Every singer – including me - likes to think he/she has an open mind, but entrenched ideas and ways can still close it without that singer realizing. An open mind will ask questions and will conduct tests and experiments. An open mind will allow those tests and experiments to lead to an answer, even an unexpected one. A closed mind will start with an answer and attempt to make all questions fit that answer.

Mental habits lead to physical habits.

If you think a piece of music is difficult to sing, it will be. Then your body will respond with tension. If you think the only way to sing a particular high note is to use muscle power, then that is the only way you will approach it. If you think intensely hard about 'solving' or 'controlling' your singing, you are likely to induce physical tension.

The more you repeat certain mental processes, the more you create muscle memory. Therefore choose carefully and precisely what muscle memory you wish to create, because it can last a long, long time. Changing existing habits and muscle memory can be difficult, but not impossible.

Take language as an example. Suppose before being a parent you were (or are) in the habit of using some swear words and other profane language, either in general conversation or when under stress. Then after having children, you consciously alter your thought patterns to avoid using that kind of language in front of your children. Where previously you had used those words almost reflexively, now they are withheld thanks to a change in your conscious brain. Changing your singing habits also starts in your mind.

Have the courage to reset your mental habits. Make the effort. Mental habits translate to physical habits. Working harder and slogging through more repetitions is not always the way forward. For example, adjusting your stance is a mental process first and a physical process second. So is changing your set-up process before singing, or trying different gestures.

Be aware that habits can become situational. If you sing in an ensemble, for example, and each week stand in the same spot in the rehearsal venue, you are more likely to develop mental and vocal habits that are repeated each time you return to that spot. The same applies to a song that you have sung many times – you have developed mental processes that are repeated each time you sing it and thus vocal habits are also repeated. Changing requires deliberate mental refreshment.

My approach to singing does not involve skills or techniques that are difficult. That is because good singing skills are not difficult. The difficult part is in the mental processes. They require the most attention and repetition. Otherwise, old muscle memory will return, particularly when under pressure.

Throw out any barriers to new ideas. Some of the approaches in this book may appear to be different from any singing coaching you have had. They certainly were like that for me. I had to take a leap of faith. It was one of the best things I have done. Convince yourself that anything is possible if you trust this approach.

Let go

When do you sing better - when you make it happen or when you let it happen?

Throughout this book, you will see me use the words *let* and *allow* many times. We want to allow good vocal production to happen with as little 'manufacturing' as possible. Trying too hard to make it happen increases tension and muscular effort, which are the enemies. Just relax and let it out.

The power of your mind

> The greatest thing I think that happened to me was one day I heard a record by the number one guitarist of all time, Andrés Segovia, and some place in this classical concerto...he made a little bobble. And I said, 'Andrés Segovia made a mistake! If he can make a mistake, who the heck am I? Who cares whether I make a mistake?' So I played with reckless abandon, didn't worry about mistakes any more. Best thing that could ever happen to me, 'cause if you worry about the music, you can't do it with conviction. So I stopped worrying about it and now I have a career that I never imagined.
>
> -------------------------------
>
> George Benson (in an interview with Aamer Haleem),
> *CTV Morning Live*, TV broadcast, May 2012.

What you think about is what your audience will think about. Are you hoping to get it right? The audience will hope you get it right. Are you thinking about executing technique? The audience will be very aware of your technique. Are you nervous? The audience will be, also. Are you baring your soul with abandon? The audience will accept and respect it willingly and gladly.

When you sing, your mind can be your greatest ally or your greatest enemy. It can set you free to succeed. It can also make you inhibited, or afraid to make a mistake, or confined to one way of approaching your singing. If your mind stops being afraid of mistakes or embarrassment or criticism, and is open to exploring your own unique way of doing things, the freedom you feel will flow into your singing.

Here is an exercise to try. Have a trusted person listen to you sing a few lines of a piece of music that is giving you some challenges. Then sing it again, but while you sing hold your hands in front of your face, palms facing out, and wave them around in large circles going in opposite directions. The pictures below provide a guide. As you sing, think only of moving your hands in sweeping circles, nothing else.

Then have your trusted person tell you which version sounded better. Most times, he/she will say the circle version. Why? Because you distracted your brain from its habitual patterns.

Here is another example that also requires a person to listen. Sing a few lines once. Then sing them again, but before you do, say out loud, 'I'm great! I'm great! I'm great!' Mean it. Then ask your listener which rendition sounded better.

How do I adjust my thinking?

You must elevate your thinking to a different level.

> ***The amateur practises until he gets it right.***
>
> ***The professional practises until he cannot get it wrong.***
>
> ***The artist practises until 'right' and 'wrong' have been transcended.***

If you have been bumping against a glass ceiling, then trying a different coach, or a different approach and mindset, might just be better than remaining convinced that sticking to your old ways will eventually work. Open your mind to new ways of thinking. Clinging rigidly to core principles can sometimes hold you back.

Get out of your comfort zone. Take a leap of faith. There is nothing to be feared by occasionally doing things differently. Sometimes we fail. Sometimes we make a breakthrough. It is how we learn and grow.

Never be afraid to start over with the basics. For some, like me, it can involve creating fundamental habits anew. Success may not happen until that occurs. Never close your mind and think you have mastered the basics. Like golfers, singers can develop problems and often must return to the fundamentals to find solutions. Some golfers and singers alike have remodeled their fundamental skills from scratch and changed their careers for the better.

Be open to what you can learn from other styles of singing and music. After all, good singing is good singing, regardless of the genre or style of music being sung. Good singing is freely produced without apparent effort, filled with honesty, and driven by passion. Good singing should involve a comfortably open throat, refreshing diaphragmatic breathing (as opposed to physically rigorous), and as much relaxation of certain muscles as is practical.

Allow new ideas to be absorbed into your personal way of doing things. Welcome them and incorporate them into your natural style. We singers are over-achievers sometimes, like when we respond literally to an idea and use too much effort. For example, a singer who is asked to raise the soft palate will likely raise it as high as possible, which is overkill and way beyond the bounds of what is natural. There is a fine line between subtle adjustment and tension. Was it absolutely necessary to raise the soft palate to its maximum height or could the singer have started with a smaller, subtler and more comfortable adjustment? Your coach may ask you to open your mouth wider, or raise your soft palate, or flatten your tongue, or inhale more deeply. But are you really supposed to 'power' those muscles? Or should you add a *hint* of the action into your own natural style?

Lastly, be patient. There are no quick fixes or tricks. Becoming a proficient artist requires years. Let expectations go and enjoy the journey. It is about the journey, not just the destination. We live in a society that moves quickly, changes quickly, communicates quickly, shares information quickly, and expects everything to be done quickly. When one is not familiar and skilled with certain fundamental skills, any help is grasped at eagerly. But many students are looking for a quick fix rather than a mindset and process that will build long-term success.

Chapter 3

My Personal Approach

This is a summary of how I go about singing, performing, preparing and practising. I remind myself frequently of these concepts. Like a golf or tennis player, it is essential to return to the fundamentals regularly. If a concept in this chapter doesn't make sense to you yet, you can read more about it in a later chapter.

Release the natural voice

The natural voice is a person's unique voice. It is the sound that just pours or spills out of a person without conscious or excessive muscular effort. It results from the simplest actions and from removing conscious thought patterns from the process. The natural voice is very much like the voice we had as infants – we released it with minimal learned actions, within our comfortable range, and we did not experience vocal fatigue from it.

Let sound out. Allow it out. Give up rigorously controlling throat and tongue muscles for air flow, pitching and shaping. Singers often use more muscle action than they need.

Learning how to allow vocal sound out without pressure or pushing or muscling is one of the hardest things for many singers to learn. It is also one of the hardest things to teach. We each have so many muscle habits we are unaware of, as well as preconceived ideas about singing techniques. But mastering how to allow sound out without excessive muscular effort provides the best possible foundation for all vocal music and sets a singer up for an extended voice life. I always recommend that a singer master the natural approach and build from there. That natural approach with very slight adjustments will allow a singer to adapt more easily to a variety of vocal genres. (The greatest exception there would be opera, which requires a much more specific and physical skill set. As a result, the operatic voice sounds significantly different from the natural voice.)

The natural voice resonates with a great deal of frontal resonance. Think of an infant's cry – the baby has no learned muscular control, yet the sound has carry and a piercing power, and the child can do it for long periods of time without becoming hoarse. As a child grows older, many factors influence vocal habits, such as language, accent, family speech patterns, environment, diet and health. Many of these factors can change a person's vocal production to become more guttural, or 'throaty', or tight, or forced, or pressed, or nasal, or 'growly', etc. In essence, during growth, maturation and early socialization, the human voice is sometimes moulded away from its natural resonant qualities. For example, my Australian accent may seem natural to me, but it developed through learning the language, and imitating the speech patterns, of people around me. It is different from other accents and indeed from vocal sounds made in other languages. Every different accent or language in the world requires different muscular actions to produce the resonant qualities and pronunciations. Some have more frontal resonance while others have more guttural qualities. When receiving vocal instruction, many singers are taught about back resonance without consideration for their spoken habits and before they have (re)explored the more natural and effortless resonance they had as small children. Most new students I encounter have excessive muscular tension in the rear of their tongues and mouths that cause a 'covered', 'muffled', 'dark', and strained sound. These singers often have difficulty developing and trusting their frontal resonance. In my experience, starting with the natural frontal resonance provides a simpler pathway, provides greater vocal flexibility and adaptability, and offers greater likelihood of long-term vocal health.

To help *you* release *your* natural voice, know what *type* of voice you have and sing the styles of music that suit it. Some voices are naturally suited to country, others to pop, or to opera, or jazz, or choral music, or other genres. Very, very few voices can do all of them, and even fewer still can do them all well. Singing music and genres that are unsuitable to your voice is not a good idea. In essence, if it encourages muscle manipulation/tension, don't do it. If it is vocally fatiguing, don't do it.

Sing within the limitations of your natural range. You cannot sing lower than your physical set up allows. Some training may help you extend your higher range a little, but there are limits there also. Accept the range that you have. It is what you have been given and it is your strength.

Front resonance and back resonance

A later chapter on placement will deal with front resonance and back resonance. Suffice to say here that in my warm-up I establish nasal resonance with a completely loose and relaxed soft palate before adjusting that palate to add some back resonance.

By the way, do not confuse nasal resonance with singing through the nose. The most powerful resonating space a singer has is above the hard palate and behind the nose. This is the nasal cavity. Singing with greater resonance and projection is not about being louder or pushing. It is about the sound carried on the exhale being guided into this amplifying chamber. In your own head, it may sound harsh, perhaps even strident, but that is not always what others hear. If you tense your tongue and throat muscles, you reduce the sound that can enter this chamber and be enhanced. If you successfully allow the sound to circulate in that nasal cavity, your other resonating spaces in the mouth and throat will be free and relaxed to do their job. However, if you concentrate your efforts on the back resonators too much, your sound will focus there and will not have the brilliance you desire.

Author's checklist for releasing the natural voice

Tension is the enemy. Any unnecessary tension can interfere with natural resonance.

- Drop your jaw hinges. Drop them to where they feel like they are just starting to unhinge. Always keep this comfortable, never forced. Let your jaw drop open with gravity. Do not push it down, just let it fall and be slack. If you are not sure it is open enough, keep your jaw relaxed as you let your head fall back and it will open more. Stay open as you bring your head back to normal position.

- A guide is to have enough space between your front teeth to insert two finger widths. But do not simply think of this as just opening your mouth. Drop from your jaw hinges.

- Feel like your jaw wants to fall. Feel like the hinges are 'well oiled'. A relaxed jaw should not be lopsided. Check in the mirror.

- See photos of jaw positions below.

Jaw dropped open.

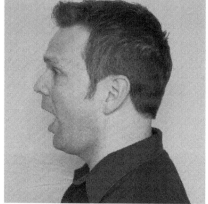

Jaw dropped open – side view.

Jaw not opened enough.

Jaw opened too far (for me, anyway).

Jaw opened unevenly.

- When the jaw is hanging open, let your tongue relax in its natural resting position. For some people, the tip of the tongue rests behind the lower front teeth; for others, the tip rests on top of the lower front teeth. If your tongue pulls backward from your teeth, it is not relaxed. Look in the mirror as you do this. Notice how much surface area you see of your tongue. Now manipulate the tongue muscles to be tense or to say 'ah' to the doctor. Much less tongue surface area is visible. The jaw should feel like the bed upon which the tongue sleeps. Practise singing keeping that tongue as relaxed as possible - without compromising basic diction - while looking at that surface area showing in the mirror.

- When warming up, let the tip of your tongue sit on top of your front lower teeth every time your mouth is open. This is an excellent exercise for preventing too much tongue tension. When your tongue is behind your teeth, it is possible to flatten it, like with a tongue depressor, using powerful muscular action. When it is on top of your front lower teeth, your ability to muscle it downward is reduced. Many singers develop detrimental habits of flattening the tongue too much and of retracting it inside the mouth.

- Allow the inhaled breath to 'drop' in with the mental image of downward motion in your lower torso. Let the air 'fall' in through that relaxed, natural space in your mouth and throat. Don't suck it in, just let it fall in. Your lower torso and diaphragm muscles will expand naturally. Avoid terms like 'pump up', 'tank up', 'give it 110 per cent', and so on. *How you breathe = how you sing.*

- Accept nothing less, not even once. It must apply for every single inhalation.

- Sometimes allow breath in through your mouth and nose simultaneously. This is an excellent exercise that some singers aim to do for all inhalations. It helps the throat muscles and base of the tongue to remain relaxed and loose.

- Stay physically loose while doing these things - shoulders, jaw, neck, pelvis (even 'bathroom muscles'), quads, knees, toes. Allow your torso to float upright on top of your pelvis. Your pelvis is the centre of your balance.

- Breaths between phrases are crucial to your performance. Use the air dropping in as inspiration for the emotion, as if discovering the words or the feelings for the first time.

- Breath flow out should be enough to ever-so-slightly warm the front of your face. Most of the time when singing, you should not need pressure much greater than that. Think of the air to rising up the front of your face.

- ***Keep the breath flowing out at a consistent rate. Every time.*** Not doing so is the cause of many problems. It is easy to fall into the trap of reducing or restricting the outward flow when singing high pitches and soft volumes. Pay attention to those ones and allow the air flow to continue warming your face.

- No glottal starts or stops ever in your breath. Allow your throat muscles to be soft and supple at all times. Breaths must fall in through this. Phrases must begin like this. Phrases must end like this with the same level of suppleness as you began them. Keep the epiglottis area loose and natural all the time. Do it when singing, when not singing, for high notes, for low notes, etc. Your throat and epiglottis must not be used as a 'pressure valve' for controlling your breath flow.

- While singing, maintain the mental image of downward motion in your lower torso. That is a mental image only; don't muscle anything.

- Mental image: Maintain a hint of a smirk in your soft palate. All the time. Sing everything through this. Keep it as a mental image only until you have mastered it. Do not muscle the soft palate up yet.

- Allow the vocal sound to flow naturally in front of your teeth all the time, never caught inside your mouth. Every activity is about consistent breath flow out and merely allowing sound out. Do not 'try' to make sound.

- A mental image for stronger nasal resonance: Imagine air coming out through your mouth and nose simultaneously. Just imagine. Allow everything to be sung through that resonance – every vowel, every syllable, every transition between syllables, every attack, every release, etc. (Remember nasal resonance does not mean singing through your nose.)

The author's personal warm-up

I apply everything in the checklist on the previous pages. I must do my warm-up before arriving at rehearsal or performance.

- 2 minutes: Make a tone through a continuous 'v' sound. No vowel, just the 'v' consonant. It sounds a little like a vacuum cleaner. Pitch should be about mid-range or just below. Continue through the entire exhale and vary it from long tones to pulses of varied lengths. Keep your lips quite loose so the sound may be a little similar to a vibrating reed on a woodwind instrument's mouthpiece.

- 2 minutes: Lip trilling (that horse noise, sometimes called 'bubbling' or 'lip rolls') with no vocal sound. Do not clench your teeth. Loose jaw, upper and lower teeth not touching.

- 1 minute: Lip trilling with sound on a mid-range pitch. Slide the pitch up and down in a siren but stay in your mid-range only. Nothing low, nothing high.

- 2 minutes: Keep lip trilling and sliding the pitch up and down, gradually widening the low and high range. Eventually expand to full range, including across your register break(s). Check you are staying relaxed everywhere.

- Your lips, tongue and even your cheeks should be tingling by now.

- Be sure you are still following the checklist from the previous few pages.

- 2 minutes: Repeat singing 'ning ning ning...' on mid-range pitches. Sing straight onto the 'ng' with the 'i' vowel zinging and popping in front of the face in a very bright tone. Focus the sound freely at your front upper teeth or your septum. Let your jaw hang down about half an inch or so. Do not keep it up. Keep your jaw and the tongue as loose as possible. Aim for the most strident sound with minimal effort.

- 1 minute: Lip trilling again. Siren up and down your full range.

- 1 minute: 'Ning...ah...' Same approach as the previous 'ning' exercise, but when the 'ng' is really buzzing (without tension), let your tongue fall away. No muscle action on your tongue, just let it fall. Let your jaw fall. Do not be concerned about shaping the vowel, just let it stay in the frontal 'ning' resonance that sounds strident in your own head. *Apply no press to your breath* – just let it flow easily. Repeat on a variety of pitches.

- 2 minutes: Same exercise with different vowels. 'Ning-ah', 'ning-ee', 'ning-er', 'ning-oh', etc.

- Reverse major triad (5-3-1) to 'ning-ah'. 'Ning-ah' each time on the 5th, the major 3rd, and the root note. Same approach as before. If your lips are still tingling from the lip trilling earlier, allow your sound to focus at that tingling area, bright and strident. No throat tension or pressure valve. To access your strong nasal (front) resonance, stick your tongue way out of your mouth for each vowel. Then do them again with your tongue in its natural resting position. Think that you are wide across your cheeks and the bridge of your nose and your eye bags. Think of having a sneer in your sound.

- 1 minute: Place your lips in an 'oo' shape, think of your inner mouth in an 'oh' shape, and siren down and up. This is based on a technique called Cuperto, which involves a small mouth space and a wide throat space. However, I prefer using the *idea* of an inner 'oh' shape rather than muscling the tongue down and soft palate up too much. Siren up and down through your full range on 'oo'. Stay as relaxed as possible, ensure the placement is allowed to be in your head/nasal resonator, and glide smoothly through your register break. (More about this exercise in the chapter 'Register Breaks'.)

- Sing an entire song replacing the lyrics with 'ning ning ning ning'. Same process applies as the 'ning' exercise earlier. Sing straight onto the 'ng' with a vowel that pops out strongly. No breath pressure.

If I do this warm-up, I should be ready for anything.

I apply these fundamental principles to my sung music. No matter how I may need to adjust the quality and placement of my voice to various styles of music, the essence of these fundamentals should remain. For example, if I must sing a more classical style that requires moderate to marked raising of my soft palate (increasing back resonance), I should do so without interfering with, or diminishing, the basics outlined above. After all, classical styles also require frontal resonance.

Other important factors when practising this warm-up

Never growl on low notes or strive to make them bigger and louder. Trust the resonance to work for you. In warm-ups, let your lowest notes dissolve into breath. There is nothing to be gained by pressing low-percentage notes out of quality.

With lip trills (sometimes called lip rolls or bubbling), if you are not sure what it means, search internet video sites like YouTube. It is an exercise that helps maintain a constant breath flow while also massaging and relaxing the vocal folds. It is particularly good to do if you are feeling vocally fatigued. Be sure your upper and lower teeth do not touch each other, keep your jaw loose, and aim for your lips to vibrate in as 'rubbery' a fashion as possible. If you feel yourself running out of air quickly, don't worry. Keep doing the exercise and your breath management will improve.

You may need to be very deliberate for a while with the process of dropping your jaw, relaxing your tongue, and then allowing the breath to 'drop' in. You may find that, when doing this, your inhale process is quite slow and interferes with musical flow. Do not be concerned. Work through it. This is totally normal and will improve rapidly with practice. But you must be deliberate and never get sloppy.

Outbound air should not be under pressure nor restricted. Indeed, this should apply to air coming in or out. The objective is to allow the natural voice to do its thing. How you inhale sets up how you sing, so the idea is to inhale with a space that is free, open, relaxed, loose, and *natural*. Then sing the same way, without muscular effort. Never put 'press' behind the sound. Let your tongue and pharynx be loose and natural.

Singing should feel super easy. In the past I was guilty of far too much muscular effort, especially in my jaw, lips, tongue and soft palate.

To make a richer or rounder vowel sound, try allowing your jaw to hang down a little further.

Be very careful when raising your soft palate with an 'egg in the back of the mouth' approach. This has its uses sometimes but overachieving produces severe tension and a covered sound.

Look for almost total physical freedom. Every exercise and every song should be done freely and easily, as if your voice just flows out with no help. It can be a bizarre feeling when first learning to do this because you think you are doing nothing, but it brings you closer to the natural voice.

Become conscious of minute amounts of tension, especially in your jaw, tongue, eyebrows, shoulders, neck, pelvic muscles, quads, knees, calves, toes, and so on. Even tiny amounts of tension can have a negative effect on your singing.

Never pitch with your chin. Sticking your chin up or out will never help with high notes, and sticking your chin down or pulling it in toward the chest will never help with low notes.

When it comes to tongue tension and relaxation, it applies to the entire length of your tongue. Your tongue is longer than it appears and its base is next to your larynx. Therefore, unnecessary tension in your tongue can cause unnecessary tension in your larynx.

Whenever you become aware of tension, deliberately relax and never try to push through. Do not 'try' to pitch the notes, just trust that your voice will go there naturally and easily with no effort.

Preparing for a performance

The following is a summary of the thoughts and processes I personally go through before taking the stage. Rather than being an instruction to you to do the same, they provide an insight into my mind backstage. You are welcome to use any of these approaches if they are helpful for you. Otherwise you may have your own routine. Use whatever approaches are helpful for you and leave you ready and focused.

A true performer does not 'own' the stage. A true performer *belongs* to the stage. A true performer is part of the stage. A true performer is one with the stage.

In performance there is nothing to prove. There is everything to *give* and *live*. I have observed many singers prepare to perform with a demeanour that says they have something to prove. Instead, I release all thoughts of proving something or gaining accolades or expecting specific results. These thoughts are distractions. I try to give freely and honestly of myself. Results will take care of themselves and singing will be much more enjoyable.

Before, during and after my warm-up, I prepare my body to be free and relaxed. Gentle yoga or stretching is wonderful for the body and carriage, especially when combined with refreshing rhythmic breathing. During such exercises, I try to quiet my mind and focus on my breathing and my contact with the floor.

If possible, an hour or so before a performance, I like to sit in the audience seats. There I soak in the dimensions and atmosphere of the performance space, while quieting and releasing any issues that have been on my mind that day. It is at this point that the performance and the space become my world. My regular world and life cease to matter for the time being. From a seat in the audience, I visualize my performance being successful. It is a ritual I go through so I can feel calm, grounded and at home in the space. It gets me mentally and emotionally in 'the zone'.

When I return to the dressing room, I stay as relaxed and physically loose as possible, keeping my mind quiet and open.

By the way, I strive never to be thrown off by the quality of the performance space or dressing room. Sometimes they are wonderful while other times they are not. That is immaterial to my preparation.

When it is time to move backstage, I begin a mental affirmation:

> *Look good.*
>
> *Breathe.*
>
> *Be you.*

I repeat this 3-point mantra to myself again and again. It is a simple summary of my approach.

Look Good

- Release tension spots - shoulders, neck, eyebrows, jaw, tongue, hips, glutes, knees, calf muscles, pelvic muscles. (Yes, even bathroom muscles!)

- Torso floats upright on top of the pelvis.

- Mental image of lifting the ears.

- Feel broad and powerful.

- Imagine bodily presence filling every corner of the entire space.

Breathe

- Be loose and natural in the jaw, tongue (entire length), epiglottis, abdominal muscles.

- Let inhaled air fall in or drop in.

- Be even and consistent with outward airflow. The rate and pressure should be just enough to warm the tip of the nose.

- Visualize having plenty of air throughout each phrase.

- Maintain a relaxed, loose and natural epiglottis. Even when not singing. Visualize this happening automatically at the ends of phrases and when preparing for the next inhale.

Be You

- Have a specific and personal story to tell with every song. The more specific and truthful, the better.

- No faking!

- Allow full release of passion and honesty. Let these out!

- Move freely and naturally.

- Do what you do. Do it *your* way. Nothing more.

- Let energy radiate outward from the core, not from the neck or the face.

- Enjoy the moment. It's supposed to be enjoyable.

The performance

The moment comes. There is no turning back. You must trust that you have prepared so thoroughly that your technical execution will be automatic and your mind will thus be free to express truth.

This is the moment a performer lives for. In this moment, the performance becomes real life and what was real life is temporarily forgotten. Nothing else matters.

Be your true self. Give your heart and soul. Anything less is letting yourself down and letting your audience down. The audience wants to see your true self. Try not to get drawn into thinking that performing means pretending or putting something on. Sometimes the primary goal may *not* be to entertain the audience. The audience's enjoyment may be a *by-product* of your *own* enjoyment and honesty.

Unfortunately, many inexperienced performers walk on stage and project a self that they *think* others want to see. That is, they 'put on' a performance. This is not only a misunderstanding of what performing means, it is a misunderstanding of music and the performing arts. To be your true self on stage requires more than repetitious rehearsal. It requires life. It requires honest reflection. It requires releasing all inhibitions. It requires releasing your conscious mind and your daily stresses so you can show the one thing that is most important to you.

What you think about is what the audience will think about. If you think about getting the notes and words correct (then you are grossly under-prepared), the audience will hope you get things right. If you become embarrassed from a mistake, the audience will also feel embarrassed or awkward. If you think about executing a technique, the audience will never see past it.

If you take the stage devoting most of your attention to your technique, it can be argued that you are not ready for performance. Perhaps ten per cent of your performance brainpower should be concentrated on technique, by mentally 'checking off' important moments and milestones. The technique work should have been done long ago.

Performance is for showing who you truly are and living your life. Performance is the time for you to release your soul, release your emotions, release yourself, and release the music. Let the music sing you; don't sing the music.

Be yourself. You already have the costume.

Afterward

Accept compliments graciously. Even if you believe you have done poorly, a compliment is still a gift. Smile and thank the person. It may be tempting to say something like, "Oh, but I mucked up that part." Never criticize yourself in front of a person who has given praise. Otherwise you reject and discount the opinion of an admirer and ally. If they enjoyed it, they enjoyed it.

Accept criticism graciously, also. Even if you disagree with it vehemently, it has a purpose. Learn to listen to criticism. Becoming a better singer takes time. Along the way, you may hear people say negative things about your singing. Unless the comments are personal, there is usually a good observation behind them. Make the adjustment, provided it does not compromise who you are or make you do something unnatural.

Take time to review your performance alone. It is easy to obsess over errors. How you react to errors and what you do about them are more important. Compliment yourself for things you did well. Make plans to correct errors so that they never happen again.

Give sincere thanks and compliments to your fellow artists. Not only might your next gig depend on a happy relationship with those artists, but spending time talking with them and asking them questions can provide insight and inspiration.

Preparing for early morning singing

Good sleep is essential to a good performance. That goes double when you must sing early the next morning. If sleeping in a hotel or motel, air conditioning can have a drying effect on your vocal mechanisms overnight and make it difficult to loosen your vocal folds in the morning. If the weather and your comfort demand that the air conditioner be on, use a cool mist humidifier in the room to counteract those drying effects. Steam humidifiers are another option, but they can make a room feel stiflingly tropical.

When you get up, drink a cup of warm to hot water with a little lemon or lime juice to clear out the overnight gunk. Follow this with one litre of water over a period of up to twenty minutes.

Eat a good breakfast. Choose food you know from experience will not interfere with your voice. Warm food is certainly helpful in cold weather. Avoid foods that are too acidic because they can remove the good mucus lining on your vocal folds. Try to minimize intake of dairy products because they may produce too much mucus. Also, keep salt intake minimal because salt has a dehydrating effect. If you are a coffee drinker, by all means have a cup, but don't be excessive with the coffee because caffeine has a diuretic effect.

Have a good shower with plenty of steam. Go through your warm up in the shower. Refer a few pages back to read my personal warm up.

Drink more water, at least another half litre.

If you can, take a brisk walk for ten or fifteen minutes, all the time with a loose, slack jaw and a loose, natural tongue, with air 'falling' in and flowing out.

Drink more water.

Do a few more lip trill sirens and 'nings' from your warm up.

You should be ready to sing.

It's not a science!

> The arts do not advance through technique,
> they accumulate through quality.
>
> ------------------------------
>
> Works of art can be inspired only by individual passion.
>
> ------------------------------
>
> Competent technique is what mediocrity has in common with
> genius, so there is small point getting enthusiastic about it.
>
> ------------------------------
>
> Clive James, *May Week Was In June*, 1990.

> Music is communication, not some kind of Olympic sport,
> and all that should matter is how you make the audience feel.
>
> ------------------------------
>
> Deke Sharon, blog entry *In Defence of Imperfection*
> www.casa.org, January 15th 2013.

> To play a wrong note is insignificant;
> to play without passion is inexcusable.
>
> ------------------------------
>
> Attributed to Ludwig van Beethoven.

Singing is not a science. It never will be. Singing is art. Music is art.

Singing is more than a mechanical process. Yet many singers allow their thought processes to become dominated by executing mechanical skills, as if mastering those skills were the ultimate goal. Indeed, many singing teachers and lessons can leave the impression that those mechanical skills are of greatest importance. There are many vocal teachers who are brilliant with technique but not as rigorous and precise with artistic development. However, do not misunderstand me. There is no doubt that repetitious practice of skills and exercises is crucial to developing good habits and appropriate muscle memory. But that repetition alone will not create a great performance. At some point, the technique must be put to work in the performance of an actual piece of music; and that music will be judged as a work of art.

As my compatriot, Clive James, said in his words quoted above, decent technique is possessed by average singers as well as great ones. That is not to say a singer should forget about technique. Rather it means that technique is not the answer to everything. All singers learn technique to some extent. That alone does not make a singer special nor does it create a work of art.

A singer's vision and passion must be of paramount importance. Technique should support the release of that vision and that passion.

If you are a 'left brained', scientifically-minded person who always thinks logically, you may have difficulty achieving your full potential in a performance art like singing. It is not impossible; far from it. But the left brain thought processes should be for mechanical actions, while the right brain should be opened and explored and enhanced.

Personally, I am dazzled and amazed by the mathematical patterns in melodies and the mathematical equations of Pythagorean tuning. They are fascinating and worthy of detailed study. But knowledge of them does not make me a better artist.

If singing were simply a matter of learning and executing a technique, the world would be filled with stars and experts. A well trained voice does not automatically provide a great experience for an audience. Too much training in rigid principles can be limiting. What the performer thinks about, the audience will think about.

A great singer is like a great actor – he will move you and draw you closer, without you hesitating or questioning. One who is exclusively a great technician can impress you, nothing more. If great technique is your sole goal, you risk distancing yourself from the human passion and emotion in the art. You must show who you are through your voice and music, not merely what you can do.

When you hear a singer, do you hear that singer's voice or do you hear her personality and soul? Do you hear the technique or the person?

Audiences assess what a singer does with music. Critics are part of an audience. They examine the artistic and emotional impact a singer has on them. Sometimes that involves discussing the singer's technique because technical flaws will block the full enjoyment and immersion for the listener. Many singers get caught up in developing the technical side to avoid such criticism, and it is prudent to do so, provided the singer remains aware that the technique must serve the art.

Always keep the artistic 'big picture' in mind when learning and refining technique. The art inspires the technique, not vice versa. Sing every piece as if it is the first and last time you will sing it. If you are not striving for your utmost experience every time you sing, why are you doing it at all? A singer – indeed any musician – must go through a process of continuous experimentation, reshaping, rethinking, re-exploring, rediscovering, redefining, and so on. That is an artistic process and a very personal one. It never stops. It is not enough to strive to perfect merely the technical process.

Physiology

The singer is usually worried by the word 'physiology'; but only because he does not clearly understand the limits of its teachings. The singer need, will, and must, know a little of it.

Lilli Lehmann, 1902.

Yes, I know. I just wrote about how singing is not a science. Singing is indeed a physiological process and extensive scientific research has been undeniably important and helpful. It is to a singer's advantage to have some understanding of the essential mechanisms and the process that takes place.

Unlike an athlete who can feel the muscles, sinews, ligaments and other tissues they develop in their training, a singer cannot feel some of the components that are used in singing. For example, the diaphragmatic muscles and indeed the vocal folds themselves.

The human diaphragm is a sheet of muscles below the lungs and shaped a little like a parachute. When a person inhales, the lungs expand and the diaphragm moves downward. The diaphragm muscles thus create pressure for the air to flow out of the lungs, up the trachea, through the larynx, and out through the mouth and nasal passages. When a person makes sound, the outward air flow vibrates the folds of tissue inside the larynx. This creates simple sound waves. When those sound waves are carried by the breath to the chambers of the throat, mouth and nasal passages, they are amplified. This last part works in a similar way to plucking a guitar string. On its own, the string vibrates but seems to make little sound. When the resonating chamber of the guitar body is added, the sound waves have somewhere to be focused and amplified. Similarly, the vibration of the vocal folds appears to emit little sound until resonating chambers amplify it.

Even that is a poor explanation of the singing process in scientific terms. As I wrote earlier, I have no intention of re-exploring the excellent research into the physiology of singing that has been conducted over many years by scholars and scientists of far greater distinction than I. A singer needs at least a simple knowledge of the physical characteristics and their function, yet should focus more upon the sensations and feelings that occur when singing.

There are so many parts of the anatomy that, when altered or moved, affect the quality of one's singing that they will be addressed individually through this book. Parts such as the tongue, the jaw, facial muscles, neck muscles, soft palate, epiglottis, and many more.

Chapter 4

General Health

Drink water. Sleep.

I cannot emphasize these enough. Drink two to three litres of plain water every day and get at least seven hours of sleep.

Do Not:

- ➢ smoke
- ➢ use drugs
- ➢ drink alcohol on performance day, nor the day before
- ➢ become a cheerleader
- ➢ shout and scream at sporting events
- ➢ go to loud bars or nightclubs
- ➢ try to be heard in noisy places
- ➢ stay up late the night before a performance
- ➢ sing outdoors (if you can avoid it)
- ➢ cough (if you can avoid it)
- ➢ clear your throat continually
- ➢ sing if it hurts to swallow
- ➢ try to talk over a cold or laryngitis
- ➢ sing higher or lower than is comfortable
- ➢ oversing
- ➢ whisper loudly
- ➢ yell or scream
- ➢ talk at a lower or higher pitch than is comfortable for you
- ➢ try to change your natural speaking voice
- ➢ talk a lot on the day of performance
- ➢ start a hydration program on the day of a performance

Do:

- get plenty of rest
- drink plenty of plain water
- speak at your natural pitch
- speak with vocal production similar to your singing
- be happy
- laugh
- avoid stress
- avoid places with foul air
- allow air to 'fall' into your torso all day long
- maintain loose jaw, tongue and throat all day long
- eat well
- avoid dairy products immediately before a performance
- treat your body with respect
- humidify your bedroom in locations with dry atmospheric conditions

Nutrition

Your staple liquid intake should be plain water. Not juice or fizzy drinks or coffee or flavoured water. Drink plain water every day, not just at performance time. Starting a hydration program on the day of a performance is too late. Proper hydration should begin weeks before a big performance, if it is not done already in daily life.

There is a saying: 'pee clear, sing clear' or 'pee pale, sing clear' or other variations. Your urine should be as pale as possible. Unless you recently consumed a lot of vitamin B, yellow urine can mean you have not consumed enough water. The brighter or darker the yellow, the more water you need.

Consuming alcoholic drinks should be minimized or even avoided. Do not believe any old wives' tales about certain alcoholic drinks being good for your voice. They are not.

As for your food, eat what you know is good for you. This includes using nutritional information we learn through our lives about the foods that are 'good' and those that are 'bad'. Use experience and sensations as a guide. Eat what makes you feel good, alert and balanced. Avoid foods that give you a quick burst of energy or alertness but then produce a 'crash' after. Notice the effect various foods have on your general well-being and on your voice. You may wish to eliminate or reduce eating foods that cause you acid reflux, excess phlegm, dry mouth, dehydration, lethargy, hyperactivity, sleeplessness, bowel irritation, a sense of heaviness,... You get the picture.

Try to avoid junk food and fast food. Such food is dreadful for general health and can cause problems for your voice, also. A poor diet can definitely affect your singing in a negative way. Good diet will not make you a more skilful singer, but it can help your vocal stamina and consistency. Avoid, or eat in moderation, foods that are heavily processed and high in salt, sugar and chemical additives. Whole, fresh foods are better for general health and better for good singing.

For me personally, I know I should eat a diet full of fresh fruits, fresh vegetables, and lean proteins.

The importance of good diet was driven home to me recently after I completed an intensive three-month fitness program. During the following three weeks, I attended a convention, went camping with my family, and enjoyed some relaxing vacation time at home. While I did not gain weight and I maintained my strength, the three weeks of 'relaxed' diet affected my mental motivation when I returned to working out. I felt lethargic during the workout, sometimes a little dizzy, and wanted to give up. If poor diet can do this to my workout concentration and motivation, imagine what it can do to my motivation and concentration to improve my singing. Imagine what it can do to my voice over a long period of time.

Physical Exercise

While physical fitness is not a prerequisite for quality singing, some improvement in your body's strength, stamina and efficiency can help.

If you are looking for exercise that supports good singing, look no further than Yoga and Tai Chi. You do not have to follow them religiously, nor is there any need to be an expert, just do something. Regular practice promotes better posture, better carriage, personal calm, confidence, and deep, healthy breathing.

Swimming is also excellent. It is low-impact exercise and it promotes cardiovascular fitness and even rhythm. In addition, sitting in a pool with the water up to chest level can be fun for gentle, casual singing. The buoyancy of the water supports your entire torso and frees your muscles.

Almost any exercise that helps you to be stronger and use oxygen more efficiently is good for your singing. However, it is best to avoid heavy contact sports. Injury can be inconvenient if it makes you miss a performance and downright devastating if it causes permanent physical or neurological damage.

Be very careful with exercises that cause you to strain or hold your breath, such as intensive working out with weights. Being stronger is certainly a noble pursuit, and can help your carriage and stamina, but straining or holding your breath can cause vocal damage. Always breathe. Expert trainers will advise you to breathe, and how to do it, when working out with weights.

My general experience has been that I sing with better quality, consistency and stamina when my entire body is in better health.

Chapter 5

Posture & Stance

How you stand affects how you sing. This applies to your body language as well as your body's balance and alignment. Ideally you want to look engaging, commanding, balanced, energized, aligned, and comfortable.

It is easy to try too hard. Sometimes you might get it just right and then your posture changes for the worse just as you start to sing.

If you are having a bad day or feeling tense and stressed, this can affect your practice and performance. To help achieve consistency, do a few relaxation exercises before your rehearsal. If it all starts going horribly wrong, take a break, relax or do something else, and try again later.

Common Misconceptions and Problems

Have you been told to press forward in your stance for performance? Some ensembles may coach this technique into singers. The idea behind it is to show readiness and energy to an audience. But watch out for problems that will interfere with your singing:

- bending at the waist
- pressing too far forward and 'gripping' with the toes
- back, neck and shoulder muscles becoming rigid
- neck and chin reaching forward
- chin reaching up for higher notes
- chin tucking down and in toward the chest for lower notes
- knees locking
- tightening the glutes and other pelvic muscles
- being unbalanced
- being limited in your movements in such positions

Posture Checklist

Find your own way of looking energetic and engaging while keeping everything free and loose. Be balanced enough so you can move in any direction.

- **Feet.** Place them approximately shoulder width apart. Your weight should be distributed fairly evenly from balls to heels but ever so slightly favouring the balls of the feet when ready to sing. Slightly. Release your toes so they are not gripping the floor. Having one foot slightly forward of the other can be advantageous, also, because you are better balanced and prepared should you need to move.

- **Calf muscles.** Keep them as loose as possible. Be sure you are not gripping with your toes or tightening your ankles.

- **Knees.** Keep them unlocked and loose. If you lock them back and straight, you are more likely to cause tension in your quadricep, waist, abdominal and back muscles. These muscles need to be relaxed for singing, unlike in dancing and some sports. If you play golf, flex your knees about 25 percent as much as you would when addressing the ball.

- **Quadricep muscles.** Like the knees, release them as much as you can. They are most likely to tighten if you lock your knees, or if you bend your knees too much, or if you lean forward at the waist.

- **Pelvic muscles.** Relax all muscles within the pelvis. That includes your glutes and pelvic floor muscles (i.e. 'bathroom' muscles). The pelvis is a weight-bearing apparatus and the centre of your body's balance. Any unnecessary tension there will spread. I hear a marked difference in vocal freedom and resonance when I remind singers to keep all muscles within the pelvis free and easy. When you inhale you should be able to feel a slight downward motion in your pelvic floor. Imagine you have a tail and ever so slightly tuck it under, just the tiniest amount. This adjustment may result in a deeper inhale.

- **Abdominal muscles.** If you tighten your abdominals and inhale, you will feel somewhat stiff and locked in place. Release them and breathe again. Try not to push them out or suck them in. Think of aligning your body rather than supporting it with muscular power. Keeping abdominal muscles released will help you achieve a better diaphragmatic inhale. More about this in the chapter on breathing.

- **Torso.** Allow your torso to 'float' freely and upright on top of your pelvis. Where the pelvis goes, your torso should float on top of it. Do not allow your torso to overbalance away from the pelvis's support. Feel broad across your clavicles (collar bones) and allow your arms and hands to hang heavily. Raise your arms straight up over your head and lower them like wings slowly back down to your sides. This gently raises the sternum without arching your back. Release your abdominal muscles again.

- **Arms.** Let them hang heavily from your shoulder sockets all the way to your finger tips. This may feel strange, especially when singing, but if you are upright in your torso and feeling broad across your clavicles, it looks engaging and even commanding. Use the heavy hanging arms idea as a start and end point when performing gestures.

- **Neck.** This area must always feel free and easy. Always. All parts of your neck, especially the nape. Let your neck and head 'float' freely and upright on top of your shoulders, with your ears above your shoulders. Imagine the back of your neck is lengthening up through the back of your skull to your crown. Frequently move your neck around fluidly to check that it is free. Any tension here will flow into your shoulders and your jaw. Become very aware of your chin and neck. Do you tilt your chin down for low notes and tilt your chin up for high notes? Do you push your neck and chin forward? Don't. These movements will hinder, not help. Train yourself to remain free and fluid in the neck and jaw at all times.

- **Jaw.** Let it hang from its hinges. Let it feel heavy and the hinges feel well 'oiled'.

- **Tongue.** Let it lie loosely in its natural resting place. Do not flatten it or retract it. Imagine that it wants to spill or slide forward and out of your mouth. Tightening your tongue will tighten your throat.

- **Face.** Keep a pleasant look on your face. Simply raise your cheek muscles and the corners of your mouth *a tiny amount*. Believe it or not, it is possible to smile while the jaw hangs open. Overusing and overstretching your facial muscles, including your lips, can cause tightness in your throat and thus your voice. Allow your eyebrow muscles to be natural, also. Some singers tighten or raise them unnecessarily when singing.

Neck Tension

Unnecessary tension in the neck is very, very common among singers. The obvious examples are when singers stick their chins and necks forward, or when they lift their chins for higher notes and tip them down for lower notes. However, there are some very subtle problems with neck tension that are not always noticeable without special attention.

Any unnecessary use of your neck muscles may place strain on your larynx and may restrict air flow and resonance.

Your neck should be upright on top of your shoulders, but always fluid and loose in this position, never tight or locked. If you collapse your neck at all, which makes your head and chin stretch forward, your larynx and trachea will not be in optimal alignment. Think that the spinal column in your neck is lengthening upward while your ears sit naturally over your shoulders and your head remains level. Try not to engage heavy effort. Remember that your neck must remain fluid, which means that as you sing, your head should be free to manoeuvre gently and subtly without any movement affecting your vocal tone.

It is extremely easy, and common, for problems to occur during the inhale process. Refer to the chapter about breathing and apply those techniques while also ensuring your neck muscles are not engaging as you inhale.

You may not be aware that your neck muscles are engaging unnecessarily when breathing or singing, so here are some photos for reference and some strategies to try.

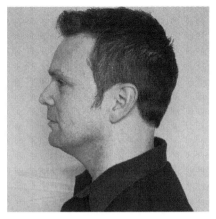

Neck in natural alignment.

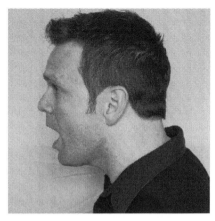

Neck tension – jutted forward to sing.

Neck tension –head tilted up.

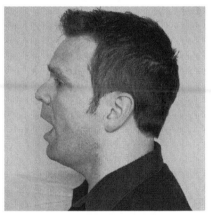

Head not tilted much, but still tense.

Neck tension – head dipped.

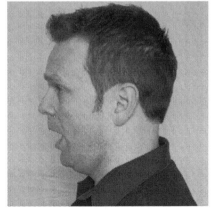

Head dipped – side view.

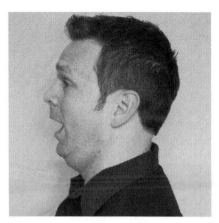

Neck retracted.

- Sit on a couch or comfortable armchair (something with generous padding) with your torso leaning back so it is resting at approximately a 45-degree angle. Ensure there is cushioning support under your neck, head and torso so nothing becomes too rounded. Feel like your torso, neck and head are melting into the couch or chair. Let all their weight be supported by the cushioning. Now sing in that position. Feel like everything is free and relaxed, especially the sensation of the head and neck melting. As you sing, any slight movement of your head or chin up and away from the couch is a telltale sign you are engaging your neck muscles unnecessarily. Trust the sound that comes out of you when you let your head and neck stay melting. The trickiest moments might be on higher notes – tricky in the mind only because you must give up muscular habits and trust what happens. (If your voice cracks or 'yodels' on higher notes while doing this exercise, let your jaw hinges fall open a little further.) You may need a friend or coach to watch you during this exercise because you may not notice any subtle rigidity in your body.

- Place your hands on your jaw and neck as shown in the photographs below. Place your pinkie fingers in front of your ears and your thumb and first two fingers on your neck. Be sure to keep your posture upright and not slumped. As you breathe and sing, you are now able to feel subtle movements in your neck and jaw muscles. Aim for those movements to be minimal or non-existent while maintaining good posture and fluidity. See photos below.

Credit and thanks to Rob Mance for showing me this one.

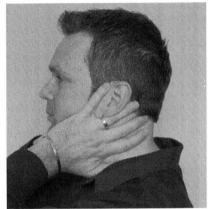

Neck tension check with pinkies above ears.

- As shown in the photographs below, place the outside edges of your palms (the fleshy, meaty parts) under the hinges of your jaw and place your palms flat against your neck. The middle fingers of each hand should almost touch each other at the back of your neck. Be sure to keep your posture upright and not slumped. If you tilt your chin up or tilt your head back, you will feel your fingers separate more. If you tilt your chin down or press it forward, you will feel your middle fingers touch. These are sure signs that you are using your neck muscles unnecessarily. Your aim is to breathe and sing without feeling your fingers separate or touch, while maintaining good posture and fluidity.

Credit and thanks to Rob Mance for showing me this one.

 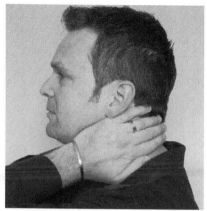

Neck tension check with palms below jaw hinges.

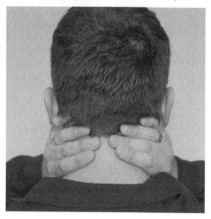

Rear view shows middle fingers close together.

How easy are these? Using these exercises, you can give your voice more freedom and resonance. When you return to standing, practise every song with a fluid neck and with the awareness provided by the exercises.

Chapter 6

Breathing

How you breathe is how you sing. Free intake of breath fosters free singing. Free expulsion of breath fosters free singing. Laboured intake fosters laboured singing. Restricted intake fosters restricted singing. Pushed, squeezed expulsion fosters pushed, squeezed singing.

Your goal is simple: efficiency. That means being able to inhale quickly and exhale slowly with consistency. It also means being able to do these things with minimal physical effort.

Do not make breathing complicated. Simplicity is often best, especially in your mental approach to breathing. As was said earlier in this book, it's all mental.

While free intake is crucial for good singing, so also is a consistent outward flow of breath. From the beginning of a phrase right through its ending, aim for the outflow to be at a consistent speed. Many singers decrease or constrict the air flow for high notes or for soft volumes. This diminishes resonance drastically. Many hesitate with the breath flow before a high note, not only diminishing resonance but also adversely affecting the flow of the music and making the upward interval sound awkward. Some singers break up the breath flow by disconnecting words from each other in staccato fashion. Unless you are aiming for a particular staccato effect, and know what you are doing, this can be most unmusical.

Common Misconceptions

Do you 'tank up' when you inhale? Do you 'suck in' the breath? Try muscling less.

Do you stand against a piano and try to shift it by the power of your diaphragmatic and abdominal exertion? I have heard of singers using approaches similar to this, if not identical. But unless you are training to be a great opera star and must fill massive concert halls without amplification and over the sound of a full orchestra, try muscling less.

Do you think breath that is placed under pressure and pushed harder will make for better singing? Do you think you must *make* it happen? If so, you will only cause problems for your singing.

Do you push and hold the abdominal muscles out when you sing? Or do you pull them in tightly to pressurize the outward flow? I used to do the former. I had been taught to do that. Since then I have learned that such heavy muscular effort causes tension in many areas of the body and thus affects vocal quality. Try muscling less.

Do you think you need Olympic-standard muscle strength to be a good singer?

Common Problems

- Raspy, noisy breathing – either you have a respiratory problem, like a cold or asthma, or the air flow is being restricted some other way.

- Chest and shoulders being lifted or even heaved.

- Breathy, thin vocal tone.

- Strained and squeezed vocal tone.

- Glottal starts and stops.

- Running out of breath regularly.

- Heavy attack and expulsion of breath on the first syllable or two of a phrase.

- Heavy attack and expulsion of air on key words.

- Outward breath placed under pressure in the throat.

- Neck and jaw muscles tightening.

- Stiffness, rigidity or tension throughout posture.

- Posture 'braced' as if preparing for impact or 'rooted' to the spot.

- Unnaturally static posture.

- Slouching posture.

Inexperienced and untrained singers often make the mistake of chest breathing. When they inhale, the chest rises and expands noticeably. Usually the shoulders rise, also. This is an understandable problem because chest breathing is what humans do during everyday life. It is also what dancers do when they dance. But chest breathing is too shallow, weak, unstable and unsupported for a singer. The result can be a vocal tone that is breathy and thin, or one that is pinched and strained.

The most common mistake singers make in regulating their outward airflow is by using throat muscles, tongue muscles and the epiglottis. We use these mechanisms all day - think how many times you swallow - thus we are often not aware of them and their subtle movements. A singer must regulate the outward airflow while maintaining a loose and supple throat. A good teacher will notice any problems here immediately. To change their habits, some singers must retrain themselves deliberately for months, even years. I had to. It is worth it.

Another common problem is releasing breath too quickly, either by it escaping too loosely or by pushing it through too forcefully. Either way, much of the breath gets wasted. Regulate the outward flow without using the throat and without tensing the tongue, neck or shoulders. Consistency in the flow is key.

Starting or ending a phrase with a glottal stop is definitely not to be done, other than very rarely for special impact in performance. Regularly closing off your trachea is a hindrance to free breathing, literally.

Inhaling

The easiest way I have found for a singer to inhale is explained below. Some of it appears earlier in this book as 'Author's checklist for releasing the natural voice'. You should also refer to photographs in the chapter about the jaw, tongue and larynx.

- Drop your jaw hinges. Drop them to where they feel they are about to unhinge. Always keep this comfortable, never forced. Let your jaw drop open as if gravity is weighing it down. Do not push it down to where muscles are stretching or tensing uncomfortably. Let your jaw fall down and hang open. I say 'let' because you mustn't force it to open too wide. Let it hang open roughly one inch and let it be relaxed. If this is not comfortable, manoeuvre and release your neck easily until the jaw position feels more comfortable. Another idea is to imagine a shelf about one inch below your chin and let your chin rest on it heavily. Feel like your jaw wants to fall and that the hinges are well 'oiled'.

- If you are not sure your jaw is open enough, keep it relaxed as you let your head fall back and it will open more. Stay open as you bring your head back to its normal position.

- A relaxed jaw should not be lopsided. Check in a mirror.

- While letting your jaw and mouth hang open, check your posture. It is easy for the relaxed 'slack-jaw' feeling to cause some drooping or sagging in your neck and spine. Stay upright, feel broad, and relax your shoulders.

- Let your tongue relax and lay loosely in its natural resting position. For some people, the tip of the tongue rests behind the lower front teeth; for others, the tip rests on top of the lower front teeth. Look in the mirror as you do this. Notice how much surface area you see of your tongue? Good. Now manipulate your tongue muscles to be tense or say 'ah' to the doctor. Much less tongue surface area will be visible. For breathing, I always prefer to see plenty of tongue surface area, whereby your tongue resembles a downward slope to your lower lip. Your jaw should feel like the bed upon which your tongue sleeps. Practise singing keeping that tongue as relaxed as possible - without compromising enunciation - and keeping that surface area visible in the mirror.

- From the slack-jawed and slack-tongued position, allow the inhale to 'drop' in or 'fall' in. Don't make it, allow it. Use a mental image of downward motion in your lower torso. Let the air 'fall' in through that loose, natural space in your mouth and throat. Don't suck it in, just let it fall in.

- As you let the air fall in, you will notice that you expand in the lower part of your torso. Good. Exactly right. If your chest has risen, you have not stayed relaxed. It is not about sucking in air or gulping down a big breath; it is about allowing the air to pass through an unimpeded space deep into your lungs and letting your abdominal and diaphragmatic muscles expand.

- Watch for, and avoid, upward movement in your chest and shoulders. But do not become fixated on this. See in a mirror which area expands more – your upper or lower torso. A tiny motion in the chest or shoulders is not the end of the world. Attempting to hold everything perfectly motionless will create unwanted tension. A heaving chest is a problem, however.

- Do not overfill your lungs. Imagine your lungs are filling like a glass of water – from the bottom up. You need fill them only about two-thirds of full capacity. That is all you require for singing. It should feel like the lower two-thirds of your torso are filled with breath, while the upper third has virtually none. That is not what happens physiologically, but that is how it can feel. Filling your lungs to their maximum will cause much tension in your chest. Try it.

- Accept nothing less, not even once. It must apply for every single inhalation.

- Sometimes allow your first inhale for a piece of music to be taken in through your nose, as if smelling a rose.

- Sometimes allow breath in through your mouth and nose simultaneously. This is an excellent exercise that some singers benefit from doing for every inhale. It helps the throat and base of the tongue to remain relaxed and loose.

- Practise inhaling this way both slowly and quickly. Either way, the process remains the same.

Repeat this many times, even the deliberate set up of the jaw, until it becomes habitual and automatic. This can take time. It may take months for you set new habits. Stick with it. You can do it at any time of the day or night, so keep repeating whenever you think of it. You do not need to be singing to practice this. You can even do it when driving the car!

Inhaling is that simple. Do not over-complicate it. Many singers work harder to inhale than they sometimes need. Unless you are singing a particularly demanding style like opera, a singer seldom needs more inhalation effort than this. By all means work hard in exercises to build strength and stamina, but you do not need to 'burst a boiler' when breathing to sing.

Exhaling

- When exhaling, maintain the slack jaw and the relaxed tongue, in the same position as for inhaling. The space in your mouth and throat should stay loose and free throughout the entire process.

- ***Breath must flow out at a consistent rate. Every time.*** I cannot emphasize this enough. Not doing so is a cause of many problems. ***Watch out when you sing high pitches and soft volumes.*** It is easy to fall into the trap of reducing or restricting the outward flow for these. This causes strain on your vocal mechanisms and an unpleasant tone.

- Breath flow out should be enough to ever-so-slightly warm the front of your face. Think of it as the warmest air you can produce and that it floats out like a cloud of breath in cold weather. If you wear glasses, think of it as enough to slightly fog or mist the lenses of those glasses. For the majority of the time when singing, you should not need pressure much greater than that. Allow the air to rise up the front of your face. Another image is to imagine a lit candle is a few inches in front of your mouth. As you exhale, you should not make the flame flicker suddenly or violently. Either it should barely flicker at all or it should be consistently leaning away from you at a slight angle.

- As breath flows out, and later as sound flows out, think of the breath flow rising like steam or vapour into the cavities of your skull. Do not push the breath out in a column of air. Allow it to rise and fill the head cavities. The diaphragm and abdominal muscles will subtly control the flow for you.

- Gently move your head and neck around. Check that your jaw remains loose.

- While exhaling and singing, maintain the mental image of downward motion in your lower torso. This is a mental image only; do not muscle anything.

- Maintain the same free space for breathing in, breathing out, sighing out, and singing out. Do not consciously engage any muscles or effort. Let it happen.

- Allow your throat muscles to be soft and supple all the time, including when you are running out of breath toward the end of a phrase. Breaths must fall in through this soft and supple set up. Phrases must begin like this. Phrases must end like this with the same suppleness as you began them. Keep these areas loose when singing, when not singing, for high notes, and for soft volumes.

- The epiglottis must not be used as a 'pressure valve' for controlling the breath flow.

- Never push your lungs to empty. If you are running out of breath, attempting to push to the end of a phrase will cause tension and make the inhale that follows tense and laboured also. Maintain the looseness in your throat, do not increase breath pressure, and stay calm. It is better to allow a split-second top-up breath to fall in than to run out completely or strain.

- Never collapse your torso when exhaling.

Other Important Considerations

Your goal is to be able to inhale quickly and then exhale slowly and consistently, all the while without excessive effort. Of course, you do not always need to inhale quickly – your first inhalation before starting to sing can take plenty of time – but you need that ability.

Listen carefully to how you inhale. An inhale that is quieter and lower in pitch is more likely to be unimpeded and deeper into the diaphragm. If it is loud, raspy and has a higher pitch to it, it is either chest breathing or has obstacles impeding it, or both.

Do not force open your throat and tongue muscles. Keep the muscles in as natural a state as possible.

Do not concern yourself with breath capacity, unless you have asthma or another respiratory disorder. Breath capacity simply means how much air you can take into your lungs. You cannot increase it. Your lungs can take in a specific limit of air and no more. However, they can take in less. Most people confuse breath capacity with singing long phrases. But you can change the rate of your exhale to last longer and be more efficient with your breath.

Beware of over-articulating when you sing. Do not allow the outward airflow to be disrupted by consonants (except for occasional emphasis or effect). Form consonant sounds lightly and nimbly - but clearly - using the tip of your tongue and the front of your lips. Be sure your consonants work *with* your consistent outflow of air, not against it.

Breaths are crucial between phrases. The inhale is part of the performance. It does not mark a stop in the action or else the flow of your music will be very disjointed. The speed, duration and nature of your inhaled breath should support the musical and emotional themes. Use the 'drop in/fall in' approach as inspiration for the emotion of the next phrase, as if discovering the words or the feelings for the first time. Allow the inhale to provide the inspiration for the notes and words you are about to sing, as if they just came to you. As the breath falls into you, feel the inspiration and courage well up within you to utter the words that follow.

The benefits of following this approach to breathing include connecting lines together, proper resetting of your body and face between phrases, keeping a song fresh, making it seem as if the words and music are spilling out of you for the first time, and a legato flow of vocal tone that is more engaging and more exciting for your audience.

Exercises

- Lie flat on your back on the floor. When you breathe, feel how your abdomen rises and falls. This is where you should breathe for singing. In this position, your breathing is natural and placed right. Free your jaw and let your body melt into the floor.

- To improve diaphragmatic strength and control, stay lying on the floor on your back and place a heavy object or book on your abdomen. Keep your body relaxed and melting into the floor. Inhale to a count of 4 and exhale evenly to a count of 16. Repeat. Do not attempt to keep the book or object as high as possible, but allow it to sink slowly and evenly with the movement of your abdomen. Then sing entire phrases in this position. You will know if your outward flow is uneven if the object on your abdomen wobbles or makes sudden movements.

- Stand with your feet approximately shoulder width apart. Bend your knees into a half crouch and do not bend forward at the waist. Raise your arms as if hugging a tree. Keep your torso upright. Now inhale. Notice that the lower part of your torso is where you fill with breath. Perfect. Reproduce this action when standing straight and normally.

- Shape your lips as if they are wrapped around a drinking straw. Inhale through that imaginary straw. Again, you will fill up in the appropriate way. Use this exercise only as a training tool for building breath strength and stamina. Do not use it for performance because it is noisy and may cause tension in your lips and through your mouth, even in your neck.

- Inhale evenly over a count of 4 and exhale evenly over a count of 8. When you reach 8 your lungs should be near empty, but maintain good posture. Repeat several times. Be sure that your outward breath flow is even throughout, so you do not run out of breath before reaching 8 (making you slow the flow rate) and so you do not have so much remaining when you reach 6 that you must suddenly speed up to expel all the breath. This will take some practice. Check regularly that you are remaining free throughout your body. Then inhale for a count of 4 and out for 12. Then in for 4 and out for 16. And so on. When performing this exercise ensure you follow all the breathing steps outlined earlier.

- If you persistently run out of breath in phrases, your diaphragm muscles may not be strong enough. In this case, do the same exercise as in the paragraph above, but do the exhale to a strong and pressurized 'sssss' sound. Use your abdominal muscles to drive the breath with sharp, explosive power that instantly makes your entire abdomen 'rock' hard. Particularly feel your solar plexus, which is the fleshy part an inch or two below your sternum. When you hiss the breath out, you should feel the solar plexus press outward strongly. If it does not, adjust how you expel the breath powerfully until it does. Check you are isolating the muscles properly and staying free in your neck and shoulders and not collapsing your torso. You will find your muscles tire quickly, but repeat regularly to improve your strength and stability. When you sing, you will not need to use such muscle power, but it is good to strengthen those muscles with exercises so they will be stronger than is perhaps needed.

- Vary the speed of your 'sssss' pulses so some are longer and sustained and others are short and rapid.

- Deep Yoga breathing. It is refreshing, rhythmic and good for you.

- When practising your singing, allow the breath flow to start for a split second before you vocalize. This will prevent a glottal start.

The epiglottis

The epiglottis is a flap of cartilage that guards the opening to your vocal folds and trachea (wind pipe). When you swallow it folds down and closes to prevent food or liquid from entering the trachea.

(When I refer to the epiglottis, often I mean the entire epilaryngeal tube and not necessarily the epiglottal flap only.)

What has the epiglottis to do with breathing? A great deal. While you cannot feel it, you use it often. Think of how many times a day you swallow and you get an idea of how much you use the epiglottis and its surrounding tissues and muscles. As a result, you have very subtle control over it, so it can also act as a brake or pressure valve for outbound air. It is where you close the trachea to hold your breath underwater. It is where the breath flow gets strained under great pressure when you lift a heavy weight. It is where you croak and growl and it is immediately next to where you clear your throat. When singing it is so important to allow this area to be natural so air can flow unimpeded.

To find the epiglottal area, hang your jaw down low and swallow a few times with your mouth wide open. Where the tissues touch and rub/close is in the area of the epiglottis. Additionally, hold your breath as if under water. Where the air is prevented from escaping is the area in question.

Notice when you sing high, you might restrict or pressurize the flow of air coming out of you, because your epiglottis is being used as a pressure control valve. Notice when you sing or speak softly, you may tend to reduce the air flow in similar fashion.

The epiglottis has an effect on vocal sound because it is right next to the larynx and the base of the tongue. Any tension in one of these areas will cause tension in the others. Tension reduces resonance. When singers use the epiglottis as a pressure valve, they make it much more difficult to produce a 'ringing' sound with strong overtones. With inexperienced singers, it is very obvious on higher notes. The outward air clearly gets caught in the tube, behind the epiglottis, and is placed under pressure so it cannot flow out naturally or easily.

My approach is to think of the epiglottis as relaxed, loose and natural at all times, so that air can flow in or out through the tube and trachea without impediment. Even when not singing, let it be loose and natural.

> *Keep your throat space loose and supple at <u>all times</u>. Begin a phrase with that suppleness and end it the same way.*
>
> *When practising your singing, allow the breath flow to start for a split second before you vocalize. This will prevent a glottal start.*
>
> *Do not start your breath flow from a closed epiglottis position. Similarly, a glottal stop – where you stop the breath flow by closing the epiglottal flap – should not be used when finishing sound or a phrase. Glottal starts and stops are abrupt and disruptive to your singing and breathing. They can be used for special effect but sparingly.*

The epiglottis is a crucial gateway. I teach singers to aim for a consistent and continuous rate of outward breath flow when singing, regardless of pitch or volume. 'Flow' is the word. When air can pass through this area freely and unimpeded, it can flow properly into the resonating cavities of the head. There the sound is enhanced and amplified. As for creating 'ring' in the vocal sound, that does not occur in the epilaryngeal tube, but the tube must be free and easy for the ring to have a chance.

Maintaining a sense of ease and natural looseness in the epiglottis and epilaryngeal tube can be a major challenge for a singer. If a singer can master this approach, he/she should feel much less vocal fatigue. If the singer keeps using the pressure valve of the epiglottis, he/she will experience fatigue frequently.

The battle is not physical. It is mental. More often than not, it is a battle against years of muscle memory. Changing mental patterns and habits is the key. Opening the mind to new thought patterns takes practice, practice, practice.

As a disclaimer, on occasions it is indeed necessary to place outward air under pressure through the epiglottis. A prime example would be posting a very long, high note. This is a very difficult technique to teach or explain. When a singer uses this technique, vocal agility is severely hampered. Changing pitch and articulating when executing this technique can be very difficult. This is another example of how the epiglottis can affect the voice.

Tongue tension and over-achieving in raising the soft palate can have a major effect on the epilaryngeal tube. As humans, we often take a piece of advice and over-achieve in implementing it. If a teacher says to raise the soft palate a little, an inexperienced singer may jack it up as if trying to inhale a golf ball. Even the tiniest amount of incorrect tongue tension or rigidity can squeeze the breath flow and reduce vocal resonance. (Refer to the later chapters about the tongue, the larynx and the soft palate.)

The epiglottis is:

- great for closing off when holding your breath
- great for using as a breath pressure valve when straining with a heavy weight
- great for protecting from food entering your trachea
- **dreadful for controlling your breath flow when singing**

When it is natural, the epilaryngeal tube will change in shape a little. It will not be rigid. It must be allowed to go where it wants. Then you have a better opportunity to allow your voice to go where it wants without muscular control.

Breath management

The general goal is for a quick inhale and slow, consistent exhale.

Do the exercises listed earlier in this chapter. Keep at them until you feel totally at ease.

If you find yourself running out of breath regularly towards the ends of phrases, there are two common problems:

1. too much is expelled in the first few syllables of a phrase

2. breath is expelled too quickly overall

Both problems involve blowing wasted breath through your larynx. They also may result in tension and pinching of your breath and sound (along with many muscle groups) in an effort to force yourself to make it to the end of a phrase. This in turn causes a more frantic and tense inhale to follow, thus causing a heavier attack on the next phrase, and the problem goes into a cycle.

To break that cycle, you need a flow of breath that is gentler and more consistent throughout a phrase. It is essential to get that flow rate in the first few syllables of a phrase exactly the same as later in the phrase. You must also let go of the idea that pushing your breath or over-emphasizing some words will make your performance more exciting. If it causes strain, pinching, or running out of breath, it is not more exciting.

Aside from referring back to the breathing exercises in this chapter, and the section about exhaling, here are some other ideas to help with breath management:

- The word is flow, not gush. Make it an even and steady flow, from start to finish, especially on higher notes and softer volumes. On the higher notes, it is easy to find yourself choking off some of the air flow as your throat muscles contract. Stay free and allow the breath to flow effortlessly.

- Let the exhaled breath rise like steam or vapour into the cavities of your head. (OK, this is a repeat of an earlier part.) Do not push the air out in a column, but allow it to float up the back of your throat and into the nasal cavities from behind them.

- Sing vowel to vowel in a legato line. That means open the vowel immediately on a note and sustain it to the last possible moment before you change to the next syllable. (If you are singing to a tempo, the vowel must be on the beat rather than the consonant.) This sustained, legato sound is exciting to a listener, no matter how boring it may seem to you in the delivery. Excitement comes from a free-flowing vocal tone rather than any explosive heaviness. You may need to overdo this legato concept in your personal practice so you do not have to be so deliberate with it in performance.

- Be careful of making consonants explosive or making them work against your flow of breath. When you form a strong consonant sound like a 't' or a 'p' or a 'k', watch that you do not build up strong breath pressure behind it before having it explode out. Let the consonant work *with* and *on* the breath instead of against it. Heavy consonant sounds release a lot of breath and also interrupt the flowing sound of your voice. When it is time to give emphasis or accent to a specific word or consonant, it is common practice to close the preceding word a little early in preparation to 'punch' the next one. Why is it common practice? Because you do it in speech. We all do, especially when we get excited. But this disrupts the outward airflow and causes tension along with an explosion of breath. Use this heavier staccato approach very, very sparingly and only for strong effect. Choose your moments wisely. Otherwise, allow the emotion and colour to be on the vowel sound. Aim for the vowel sound of the preceding word to flow *into* the key word and use a change of tone or colour to provide emphasis. That way your breath flow will remain consistent, your lines will be more musical, your music will have better forward motion, your audience will be less jolted by broken sound, and you reduce the risk of running out of breath by the end of the phrase.

- Finish a breath or phrase the way you started it: free, open and relaxed. It is easy for the vowel sound to deteriorate or close down as your breath runs out. Keep your jaw loose and open, and think 'open' in all the resonating spaces of your head as you finish a phrase. Do not physically manipulate muscles in your mouth, throat or neck; just think 'open'. Then you are in excellent position for the next inhale.

- Breathe where you need, provided it is sensitive to the music or story. It is not a contest to see who can sing the longest phrases or hold a note the longest. You do not drive a car until it runs out of fuel. At least, I hope not. You stop before that and fill up. And you do so at an appropriate place, not just anywhere. Do the same with your singing. Breathe when you need, but make good musical choices. Especially avoid breathing in the middle of a word. Set your breathing places, along with some emergency places, and remember them. Make smart and achievable choices. Even if you sing in an ensemble where the conductor or director sets the breathing points, you still have a personal responsibility to remember the plan.

- Never push until empty just to finish a phrase. This causes awful tension, sounds dreadful, and creates a cycle where the next inhale will be tense and thus the next phrase will be tense and so on.

- You may have heard your hero sing a phrase or note for ages. But you are you. Deliver the message of the music. Do not be distracted from delivering your message.

- (A repeat from before.) If you persistently run out of breath in phrases, your diaphragm muscles may not be strong enough. In this case, do the pressurized 'ssss' exercise mentioned a few pages back. Use your abdominal muscles to drive the breath with sharp, explosive power that instantly makes your entire abdomen 'rock' hard. Particularly feel your solar plexus, which is the fleshy part an inch or two below your sternum. When you hiss the breath out, you should feel the solar plexus press outward strongly. If it does not, adjust how you expel the breath powerfully until it does. Check you are isolating the muscles properly and staying free in your neck and shoulders and not collapsing your torso. You will find your muscles tire quickly, but repeat regularly to improve your strength and stability. When you sing, you will not need to use such muscle power, but it is good to strengthen those muscles with exercises so they will be stronger than is perhaps needed. Vary the speed of your 'sssss' pulses so some are longer and sustained and others are short and rapid.

Chapter 7

The Jaw, Tongue & Larynx

As beauty and stability of tone do not depend upon excessive pressure of the breath, so the muscular power of the organs used in singing does not depend on convulsive rigidity, but in that snakelike power of contracting and loosening, which a singer must consciously have under perfect control.

Lilli Lehmann

The jaw, tongue and larynx are inextricably linked. The base of the tongue, which you cannot see, is attached to the top of the larynx. The hinge of the jaw is also close to the larynx and to the rear half of the tongue.

Tension in one either causes tension in the others or is caused by tension in the others. The result of that tension is an unpleasant tone with reduced resonance.

A relaxed jaw and tongue will produce a relaxed and free larynx.

Unnecessary tongue tension is one of the most common problems for singers. Many are not aware they are using their tongue muscles more than they need. Good coaching will identify the issue and provide strategies. The challenge then is to create new habits and erase old muscle memory.

Letting go of jaw tension, tongue tension and 'throat tension' can be very difficult. Many singers use these for shaping vowels, pitching notes, and for holding extended notes steady. But excessive muscle tension is detrimental to vocal health, vocal stamina, tone quality, musicality, and – ironically – detrimental to control.

Trace your finger from just above one jaw hinge (near your rear upper molars), under your chin to your Adam's Apple, then over to the jaw hinge on the other side. This is the most common 'band of tension' for singers and speakers. I call it 'The Quaker Beard' because, like the beards in photos of old-style Quakers, it runs under the chin and across the throat from jaw hinge to jaw hinge but without a moustache. As you sing, feel this band with your hand or finger to identify where you are tensing. Release them and... let it out!

Common Problems

- Forcing or pressing the voice.

- Opening the jaw unevenly.

- Opening the jaw too far.

- Not opening the jaw enough.

- Jutting the chin and/or neck forward.

- Stiffening or locking the jaw.

- Tongue being pushed down and flattened like with a tongue depressor.

- Tongue twitching or moving around the mouth during singing.

- Tongue retreating and/or retracting.

- The rear and the base of the tongue being made rigid.

- Making an excessively deep furrow along the centre of the tongue, from front to back.

- Larynx leaping around suddenly and violently with changes in pitch.

- Larynx being forced to stay down.

- Over-articulating.

- Articulating too much with the rear of the tongue and mouth.

- Temporomandibular joint disorders (TMD or TMJ). If you do not know what this is, it probably may not affect you.

The Larynx

Feel your Adam's Apple. You are feeling the protective thyroid cartilage that encases your larynx. The technical term for the Adam's Apple is the Laryngeal Prominence. It is more visibly noticeable in teenage and adult males than females because a male's larynx grows significantly larger during puberty, which causes the voice to 'break' and results in deeper vocal pitch.

Sound is simply vibration. The larynx's purpose is to vibrate. Breath passes through it, vibrates the tissue folds, and those vibrations then continue into the resonating chambers. On their own, the vibrations in the larynx make very little sound, just like guitar strings vibrating appear to make very little sound until the guitar's hollow resonating wooden body is added. Therefore, do not think that singing happens in the larynx. Singing really happens in the mouth and teeth and resonating chambers of the skull.

Have you ever been taught you must keep your larynx down at all times when singing? Some singing teachers are adamant that it must be kept down. I recommend caution and some flexibility with this approach, mostly because it is often poorly taught and explained, with the result that a singer forces the issue and creates unnatural, over-muscled rigidity. The idea has a noble purpose but try not to become hung up on it. Humans are overachievers, remember? A consistently lower larynx position is required for classical styles of singing. In other styles, the larynx may either be higher or else will fluctuate naturally.

Whatever you do, it should always feel comfortable. Becoming hung up about keeping the larynx down can make you tense. I recommend focusing on *elasticity* and *freedom* in the area of the larynx. When it is free, it will stay in a lower position most of the time, but will also move around in a gentle and subtle manner quite naturally. Fighting against this causes tension. However, do not let it jerk and jolt around all over the place in a sudden or violent fashion. Find what is natural and relaxed.

Much depends on an individual's unique vocal structure and the style of music being sung. Personally, with my lighter vocal quality (I mean lighter in timbre, not necessarily volume), keeping my larynx down has been detrimental by causing me tension, fatigue, throat soreness, and an unattractive tone. I have been more successful focusing on freeing the base of my tongue. After all, the base of the tongue and the larynx are inter-connected.

Larynx Strategies and Exercises

- First let your jaw and tongue be loose and relaxed at all times. This is vital.

- When you sing, feel your larynx (Adam's Apple) with your finger. Let it be free.

- As was outlined in the previous chapter, using the muscles of, and around, your epiglottis to control and pressurize your outward air flow is deadly to your vocal quality and vocal stamina. Keep your throat muscles loose and natural so breath may pass in and out unimpeded. The epiglottis must feel like a permanently open gateway.

- Then follow the exercises and strategies for the jaw and the tongue.

The Jaw

Strategies and Exercises

- Always breathe when doing these exercises.

- As mentioned earlier, drop the hinges of your jaw to where they just start to 'unhinge' and let the breath 'drop' in. Do this until it becomes habit and occurs for every inhalation. The following photographs may provide a guide.

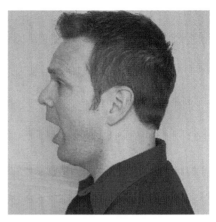

Jaw dropped open from its hinges.   *Jaw dropped open – side view.*

Jaw not opened enough.   *Jaw opened too far (for me, anyway).*

Jaw opened unevenly.

- If you are anything like me, and many others, you will have jaw tension at various times of the day. Mine is often particularly bad when I am driving or concentrating. The tension could be obvious like clenching or less obvious like the jaw being held still and rigid. This causes the muscles to remain tense and also affects your breathing.

- Consciously allow your jaw to hang open loosely from its hinges at any and all times. Let the breath fall in and out. Walk around and drive around doing this. It is a most beneficial habit to form.

- Do you grind your teeth in your sleep? See a medical or dental professional. The muscle actions and tension are not healthy for singing. Simple solutions are available. If you are serious about your singing, you will do something.

- Allow your jaw to hang open, then tilt your head back while leaving the jaw hanging. Feel the jaw hinges stretch gently. Maintain that position for 30 seconds. Bring your head back to its normal position and maintain that feeling of a loose jaw. Retain that sensation when singing.

- A loose jaw and a legato line have a great deal in common. Let your jaw feel heavy whenever possible. Practise letting it fall open instantly and heavily to each vowel sound in a line of music. During your personal practice it is okay to feel like you are overdoing this to the point where you think words are not entirely clear. Overdoing it helps establish a habit more quickly. In this exercise, sing consonants with a flip of your tongue only. Use the tip of your tongue, form every consonant sound toward that tip, and let it return instantly to a resting position.

- Sometimes you do not need to lift up that heavy jaw when changing from one syllable to the next. All you may need is a flick of the tongue tip and to allow the jaw to remain resting. Practise singing 'la-la-la-la-la...' in the mirror letting only your tongue move. Move your jaw around while doing this, as described in the next point. Try other versions such as 'na-na-na...' or 'lee-lee-lee...' or 'day-day-day...', etc.

- Grip your chin with your forefinger and thumb. As you sing, gently wiggle the loose jaw up and down and sideways. Gently. It should always feel easy to wiggle.

- Loosen jaw tension during rehearsal with a slight chewing motion.

- Drop your jaw. Place your finger on your chin. Sing a scale or line of music to 'Yah-yah-yah...' without your finger being moved around. Do it again with your tongue sticking out.

- Learn to isolate movement in each lip. In front of a mirror, drop your jaw and try to move your upper lip up and down in total isolation. Be careful that you do not squint or 'scrunch' the muscles beside your nose. It may take time before you discover the muscles of the upper lip. Then do the same exercise trying to move the lower lip in isolation. Be careful not to move your jaw or to tighten it.

- When you are doing jaw exercises and singing with a loose jaw, watch in the mirror to see if you have a habit of twitching your upper lip or nose muscles. The upper lip twitch is a sign of slight lip tension which can shift easily to your jaw and tongue.

Upper lip raised.
Do not breathe like this

Lips tense.

- Learn to isolate your jaw movements from the rest of your facial movements and expressions. Refer later in this chapter to the 'ventriloquist dummy' idea in the section about the face.

- Be very careful when shifting your jaw from side to side. Some people have no problem with such movements, while others risk a jaw becoming locked out of place. Focus more on it dropping or 'swinging' down and up freely.

The Tongue

The tongue is the bane of many singers' existence. An overly tense tongue restricts the channels for your breath and voice, and thus restricts your vocal resonance.

Essentially, the less your tongue does when you sing, the better. Stop over-achieving with it. It does not need to be used with Olympic-level muscle power for pitching or shaping or anything. You *do* need subtle control over the muscles, no question. You *do* need to learn how to:

1. use the tongue in extraordinarily subtle and tiny movements,

2. make those adjustments and movements as relaxed as possible, and

3. execute those subtle movements in isolation from other muscles in and around the throat.

Release, relax and rest your tongue at every opportunity. That means the entire length, right down to its base near your larynx. Too many singers use their tongue muscles way more than they need for vowel shaping and pitch control. Use it just barely enough to enunciate. Otherwise relax it and let it stay out of the way naturally.

Train your mind to let it rest as much as possible. Your vocal health and stamina will thank you.

Of course, classical singers flatten the tongue down and raise the soft palate to increase resonant space. This is indeed a good thing to do. I can do it better now than I ever used to, even though doing it more than a fraction does not suit my voice. However, in the inexperienced singer who has not yet mastered the natural voice, the tension of the tongue and soft palate muscles will focus the vocal sound in the area of the manipulation. The rear of the mouth is all soft tissue which darkens and even 'muffles' sound. Many have been told to sing as if they have an egg in the back of their mouths, but without mastering the release of the natural voice this often results in a covered, 'swallowed', 'dark', and unpleasant sound.

> *I encourage singers to master the natural tongue position and the natural 'ring' in the nasal resonators before attempting to open the soft palate and tongue space. Mastery of the former means the powerful frontal resonance should not disappear when applying the latter.*

Tongue Strategies and Exercises

First get your tongue into good position. Find the position in your mouth that feels comfortable and produces your best sound. You will definitely need a coach or a trusted ear to help identify your best sound.

- Drop your jaw open, as described earlier. Let your tongue rest in a loose and completely unforced position. Look in the mirror. You should see plenty of your tongue's front surface area, as if the front of it is like a ramp sloping down to your lower lip. If you do not, you are tensing the rear of your tongue. A natural tongue position should be with the tip resting behind the front lower teeth or even on top of them.

- See photos on next page.

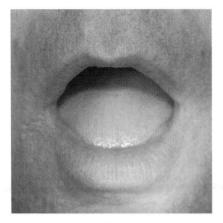 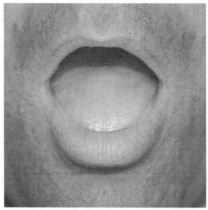

Tongue tip behind front lower teeth.   *Tongue tip on top of front lower teeth*

Notice how much surface area you can see of a relaxed tongue.
These two positions may look the same, but the subtle difference is noticeable when singing. Use what is most comfortable for you.
NOTE: My tongue in these photos is not near, or in contact with, the roof of my mouth or my soft palate, despite any possible appearance to the contrary.

- When you sing with your most natural voice, you should be able to see in a mirror plenty of front surface area of your tongue. A relaxed tongue is not flat like a table, but has a convex curve all the way to the tip. Be very wary of flattening the tongue, or dropping it down, or retracting it, or bunching it. Tiny adjustments here and there may, and will, occur, but dramatic changes are a danger sign. Experiment with the resonant sensations with each vowel sound, so that each feels like it is vibrating and penetrating the same spaces of your head. You may even find that the strongest resonance on some vowels occurs when you do not drop the back of your tongue as far as you have done previously. For example, I once sang my 'ee' vowels with deliberate internal mouth space and my tongue depressed. However, I sounded covered, dark, muddy and forced. Now my tongue surface area is easy to see, my jaw is loose, the sides of my tongue may be lightly in contact with my upper middle molars, and my sound is cleaner, more focused and stronger. Experiment yourself.

- As you sing extended notes, watch your tongue in a mirror. If it flattens so far that you can see your uvula (the tissue dangling at the rear of your mouth), it is possibly too tense. If the length of your tongue has a deep valley or furrow along its middle from front to back, it is possibly too tense.

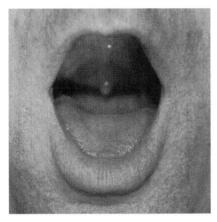 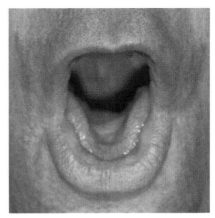

Flattened with "tongue depressor". *Tongue deeply furrowed*

Believe me, both of these positions were very tense when photographing them. Tension was strong in my tongue, lips, soft palate, jaw, and neck.

Your tongue may not become as deeply furrowed as the photo on the right. Perhaps it develops more of a 'crease' or depressed line along its length. Tension can be subtle and small as well as dramatic and large.

- Your jaw should be like a bed for your tongue. Whenever your jaw opens and drops, your tongue should lie comfortably and naturally on its bed. As I teach many singers, my initial concern is removing unhealthy and unnecessary habits. I help them rediscover the natural voice. Often this means thinking less about space at the rear of the mouth and more about space between the teeth while maintaining a natural, loose tongue position. (Refer to sections about dropping the jaw hinges open or resting the chin on an imaginary shelf.)

- Does your tongue retract and bunch up toward the rear of your mouth? If so, seek some coaching. You are accustomed to using far too much muscle power in your tongue movements. It is affecting the position and alignment of your entire vocal set up and is affecting every sound you make.

Correcting this habit can be a challenge. At every opportunity, let the tip of your tongue rest naturally against your front lower teeth, or on top of them if that is more natural/comfortable.

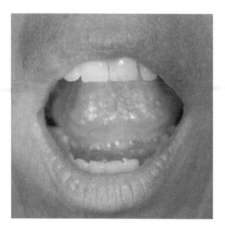

Tongue retracted and bunched to expose the floor of the mouth between the front teeth and the tongue.

- When warming up, let the tip of your tongue sit on top of your front lower teeth for every vowel sound. This is an excellent exercise for minimizing tongue tension. When your tongue is behind your teeth, it is possible to flatten it with powerful muscular action, like with a tongue depressor. Try it. But when it is on top of your front lower teeth, your ability to muscle it down is reduced. It is easy to develop the habit of flattening the tongue too much and of retracting it inside the mouth. *(Note: When my jaw falls open, the comfortable default position for my tongue to rest is on top of the teeth. I often do it when performing, also. You may be the same or you may not. Do what is natural and comfortable.)*

- Place an upright finger under your chin and find the soft tissue between the bone of your chin and your Adam's Apple. See photograph below. Now swallow. You should feel a muscular action push your finger downward. That is the digastric muscle. With the finger there, retract or flatten your tongue. You should feel a similar press downwards on your finger. When you make vocal sound, aim for that muscle to stay soft and pliable. If it tenses and pushes your finger down, you have activated your tongue muscles. Your tongue does not need to work so hard. You may have to sing often with your finger there in a bid to be consistent, but the less work that muscle does, the better.

Feeling for freedom or tension in the digastric muscle.

- Sing an 'ah' vowel with your tongue sticking out as far as possible. Keep it directed straight forward and shaped to a point, always stretching. Keep a pleasant look on the rest of your face, even smiling. You will get strong front/nasal resonance and the weight on the digastric muscle will be lifted. Of course, you won't be able to articulate or enunciate properly, but you will have plenty of forward placement and be unable to depress the base of your tongue in a tense and muscular manner. Then sing other vowel sounds. You should be able to find a forward placement for each and also be able to make every vowel sound distinct. Try to reproduce the same resonant sensations (and the looseness in the digastric muscle) when singing normally. It can be difficult to establish this new habit, but it is well worth it.

- For every vowel you sing, think of your tongue as loose and almost spilling forward out of your mouth.

- Experiment with how much or how little space you have between your relaxed tongue and the roof of your mouth. Do this by varying your jaw position subtly and trying different vowel sounds. Personally, for example, when I sing an 'ee' vowel, my tongue may even lightly touch the insides of my first molars, and the space between my tongue and the roof of my mouth is much narrower than I had once thought allowable.

- Warm up, and even rehearse, with your tongue and jaw so loose and relaxed on vowel sounds that you feel like you may almost drool.

- When singing higher notes, beware of tensing the rear of your tongue and flattening it strongly. You do not need to do this in order to pitch or shape notes and vowels. Practise those notes so they resonate further forward in your face and even in front of your teeth. This is a sensation in your face rather than any forced action. Some people feel like their facial bones are 'buzzing' or like glass is shattering in their heads. I feel some of those sensations, along with the feeling like I have air swirling through my sinuses. (I may or may not have air swirling there, but it sure feels like there is.) If necessary, try those notes with your tongue sticking out as far as possible, as described earlier, and then reproduce the sensation with your tongue in normal position.

- Say tongue twisters repeatedly. Some examples are listed below. Use your tongue as little as possible to say them clearly. Mastering tongue twisters teaches subtle, nimble and quick isolation of different tongue muscles. Even though these are spoken activities, do the same things as you should when singing: keep a loose jaw and keep a consistent flow of air through the words. Do not over-articulate the consonants; the breath flow must be consistent throughout as the consonants emerge *on* or *with* the breath instead of against it. More in the next section on articulation.
    - Red leather, yellow leather.
    - Red lorry, yellow lorry.
    - Eleven benevolent elephants.
    - Good blood, bad blood.
    - Unique New York.

- Betty Botter bought a bit of better butter.
- The sixth Sheik's sixth sheep is sick.
- Worldwide Web.
- Santa's short suit shrank.

- There will be more about placement and frontal resonance in a later chapter. For now, remember that unnecessary tongue tension reduces resonance.

- Be aware that manipulating your soft palate also moves the base of your tongue. When a singer reaches an appropriate skill level with the tongue issues listed here, then I encourage him/her to experiment with the soft palate position. *But...* in miniscule amounts. A millimetre at a time. If it feels difficult or causes fatigue, that singer should ease off.

Articulation

Common Problems

- Tongue exertion and tension, particularly at its base.
- Over-articulating.
- Articulating too far back in the mouth.
- Consonants under pressure, thus impeding breath flow.
- Stiff jaw.
- Lip tension.
- Under-articulating/slurring.
- Choppy singing.
- Tempo increasing.
- Resonance changing dramatically from one word to the next.

Strategies and Exercises

- Always start with the legato line, so your singing flows from one vowel sound to another in what seems like a constant stream of sound. It is simply more musical and more engaging for an audience. Believe it or not, it is possible to articulate clearly when doing this. The articulation has less to do with forcing or clipping, and more to do with being nimble and agile. Vocal sound that is clipped and chopped is rarely more exciting than one that is continuous.

- Do not sing onto the consonants. Do not bounce onto them. This can take deliberate mental effort. Since we were infants, songs were sung to us in a very choppy style. Think of the opening line to *The Wheels on the Bus Go Round and Round* and how they are usually sung to small children. You can bet that most times the vowel sounds are very short, the 'u' in 'bus' would be very short, the 's' in 'bus' would be pressurized and too long. Now think of singing *Mary Had A Little Lamb*. It would almost always have been sung to you, or by you, with the 'i' vowel very short every time in the word 'little' and the vocal sound stopping momentarily at the 'tt' sound. In essence, the consonants have become the targets instead of the vowels. Delivering a legato line without attempting to bounce onto consonants can take practice because it goes against many of our earliest formative memories of singing.

- Use the tip and front sides of your tongue to articulate lyrics. Do not use the rear or base of your tongue.

- Form consonant sounds lightly and nimbly, but clearly, at the tip of your tongue, your front teeth and your lips. Be sure your consonants work *with* your consistent outflow of air, not against it. Beware of forming some too far back, such as 'K', 'L', and 'R'. Even these can and should be formed at the very front and on the outward breath flow.

- When forming words, in general the tip of your tongue should stay at or near your lower front teeth. Yes, different sounds and pitches require different tongue involvement, but the point is to operate the tongue at its front end and keep the back of it from bunching or bulking up.

- For any consonants that involve your tongue touching the roof of your mouth, try to make that contact on the hard palate instead of the soft palate. For example, consider how you form the 'K' sound. Imagine the breath that follows it carries a vowel sound. If you form it like 'kah', your tongue will make contact with your soft palate, which is too far back. Now try it as if it is 'ki' (with the same vowel sound as in 'kit'). For this version, your tongue will make contact with your hard palate. Better and easier. Even with the 'ng' sound, which usually makes the tongue touch the soft palate, think of it being as a far forward as possible.

- Adapt how crisp or heavy or light your articulation should be according to the genre, the venue, the acoustics, the sound system, and so on. But adapt without compromising that all-important flow of sound.

- Repeat over and over "The tip of the tongue, the teeth and the lips". Here are a few tips to make this exercise effective:

  o the words indicate where the focus must be

  o try to keep your outward breath flow consistent, even when forming hard consonants like 't'

  o extend the vowel sounds and join them together

  o over-articulating will disrupt your breath flow, so make the consonants work with/on the breath and not become pressurized or explode out

  o maintain a loose jaw, so the front of the tongue may dance

  o the more nimbly and effortlessly you can do this exercise, the better for your singing

  o apply these approaches to music where you must deliver words quickly – you will find it works beautifully to maintain a flowing legato line.

- Choose carefully when to produce more plosive consonants or when to sing through consonants. Do so for effect or for a specific reason. After all, word sounds can provide emotional impetus. In such a case, sound and use the *singable* consonants like 'n', 'm', 'l', 'r', and 'ng'.

- Be very wary of *unsingable* consonants. When you use those too heavily, the effect may sound like singing note to note, instead of singing long lines.

- Practise dropping your jaw open immediately to vowels. Get to the vowel sound instantly and sustain it for as long as possible before changing. This may seem a boring way to sing when you practise, but it sets up good habits and reminds you that there is more excitement in the singable sounds.

- When practising the 'boring' approach above, be sure you get cleanly to each note and vowel. Avoid slurring and sliding. Ensure your jaw gets every chance to drop open and rest on its shelf.

The Face

Common Problems

- Dead face.
- Frowning, or the 'thinking' face.
- Smiling too much.
- Facial contortions.
- Stiff facial expression.
- Lip tension.
- Pushing lips forward off the teeth too far and over-shaping.
- Jaw stiffness.
- Chin jutting.
- Eyebrow tension.
- Flaring of the nostrils.
- Tension flows into other areas like the neck and shoulders.

Many singers make the mistake of thinking they must be facial contortionists. However, a good singer is one who looks and sounds natural.

Dead face. Everything drooped.

Frowning.

Thinking face. (Or is this maniacal?)

Lips tense. Made the tongue tense.

Strategies and Exercises

- First, go through the earlier chapters and sections about freeing your body, posture, breathing, neck, jaw, and tongue. If you are tense in these areas, it will show in your face.

- Maintain a pleasant look on your face as a default that is neither drooped nor lifted too far.

- It *is* possible to smile while maintaining a loose, hanging jaw. The muscles above your mouth can be moved in isolation from the jaw.

- An extreme, but easy to understand, example is a ventriloquist's dummy. The face, especially at the cheeks, is permanently lifted, as are its mouth corners, while the mouth mechanism flaps up and down easily. Without going to the extreme level of one of these dummies, keep your cheeks slightly lifted (a millimetre or two) while your jaw can flap up and down with no resistance or friction and without disturbing your facial expression.

A ventriloquist's dummy.

Jaw free, slight lift in cheeks.

Smile with lifted cheeks. Perhaps a little extreme, but you get the idea.

- Imagine a line has been drawn from the corners of your mouth to your ears. Think of that line being buoyant. Keep your jaw loose and feeling heavy. You do not need to put on a huge and cheesy smile, but just feel pleasant buoyancy at the corners of your mouth and in your cheeks.

- When lifting your cheek muscles slightly, beware of raising your upper lip too far.

- Imagine lifting your ears.

- As you become comfortable with these sensations, you can start to smile more broadly as the mood or emotion permits, but always maintain that free jaw.

- Even when performing music that is filled with sad or painful emotions, the slight lift of the cheek muscles is still appropriate. Rather than appearing like you are smiling through those emotions, your face will appear alive and engaging.

- Check your neck. Relax it and keep it feeling fluid.

- Be careful when overly rounding your lips for vowel sounds and pushing them forward off your teeth. (Some people call it the embouchure, likening it to the lip shapes created by players of certain instruments.) Refer to the photographs below. Every singer is different. Something that works for one does not always work for another. A little lip shaping can be very helpful for vowels like 'oo', 'oh', and 'er'. Just be aware that too much places strain on your jaw, tongue and larynx, and will darken and 'cover' your sound by restricting front/nasal resonance. Additionally, thrusting the lips forward too far into a rounded shape can make facial expressions look decidedly unnatural. Many barbershop harmony singers were taught for years to thrust their lips forward and round them at all times. I find it detrimental for my 'ah' and 'eh' and 'ay' sounds. I am not a fan of it for 'ee' sounds either. But I will not totally rule out the approach. As I said, every singer is different. Find what is comfortable, unforced, and sounds free and consistent to a trusted ear. A subtle shaping can help, but remember that vowel sounds do not originate in the lips.

'Embouchure' lips. Tension spreads to other areas.

Another example 'embouchure' lips. Tension spreads to other areas.

Note: When some singers raise their cheeks slightly and sing with a free, loose jaw, they may *look* like they are pressing their lips forward off their teeth. I have had an observer comment to me that he thought I was creating the 'embouchure' with my lips during performance. However, it was purely incidental. I made no conscious attempt to push my rounded lips forward. Instead I was focused on comfortably raising my cheeks and the imaginary lines from the corners of my mouth to my ears.

Rhythm

Give up the idea that you must *make* rhythm happen and *make* it exciting. *Feel* the rhythm through your body and *allow* it to flow.

By all means, in the learning stage you should break rhythms down and learn them by slow, careful and deliberate repetition. By all means, when you start singing at the desired tempo, use a metronome to be sure you are accurate without speeding up or slowing down. Just remember that these approaches are for learning only. When you have learned and mastered the rhythms, you must release those mental patterns that you used for learning them and begin feeling the rhythms in the music and how they fit with your natural way of singing.

Use your body and not your brain. The body is excellent at rhythm. The brain is terrible at it. The harder you think about rhythm and try to intellectualize it, the harder it becomes. Let your body move in your own unique way. Lose all self-consciousness. Those who are best at rhythm show it naturally through their whole bodies.

It is very easy to over-emphasize rhythm. The most common ways are to accent downbeats heavily and to close off words early to separate them in the hope this will make the rhythm more distinct and exciting. However, such a 'pounding' or 'chopping' approach rarely makes the rhythm more exciting, unless the singer is a skilled vocal percussionist. The key elements are a continuous flow of breath and a continuous flow of sound. It *is* possible to have a connected flowing sound *and* clear rhythm.

Occasionally, a more staccato approach is appropriate or provides momentary contrast, but all too often it is used too much and results in a broken, jerky sound.

Be sure that every syllable in the rhythm has a tone and pitch to it. When singing faster or more complex rhythms, it is easy to break the tonal flow and not sing a proper note on some shorter syllables. The rhythm serves the line.

When some singers first try producing good rhythm with a flowing and connected tone, they can end up overdoing it and slurring their words. A relaxed tone and a relaxed tongue and jaw do not mean lazy. Where the beat falls is where the vowel sound should fall, not the consonant. The tip of the tongue can be agile, nimble and crisp in its movements without interfering with the breath flow. Use that tip. Articulating further back in the mouth will make rhythmic work more difficult. Work *with* the breath flow, not against it.

Refer to the section earlier about the tongue.

Another issue that can arise when attempting to connect flowing tone together is that every syllable in the line sounds like it is receiving equal emphasis and weight. That may sound reasonable when singing *Happy Birthday*, but would make the flow and rhythms of *Birdland* or *Joshua Fit the Battle of Jericho* sound ploddy and heavy. Singing a continuous tone does not mean a heavy or blatted vowel for every syllable. Some syllables, when we speak them, receive a neutral vowel sound – the unstressed 'schwa' – and there are moments in music and rhythm when that sort of speech application should apply.

Rhythm takes time and practice. The more you immerse yourself in different forms of music, and the more you allow rhythm to flow naturally through your body, the better your rhythmic singing will be. It would be nice for me to go into greater detail here, but there are so many different rhythmic devices in music that I could never cover them all and the vocal approaches to them. Suffice to say, build your foundation of a free flowing stream of sound and allow rhythms to work *with* that more than against it.

Chapter 8

Soft Palate

We singers are supposed to raise the soft palate, right? But *how high*? That depends sometimes on the genre of vocal music. Being told to arch it as far up as possible is detrimental to 90% of singers because it is forced and unnatural.

A singing teacher will rightly say to a singer to raise the soft palate. Unfortunately, even when asked to raise it slightly, an inexperienced singer will over-achieve and raise it as high as possible in a tense and unnatural manner.

Some lifting of the soft palate is often helpful in singing because it provides some back resonance to the voice. It increases the space through which breath passes and can enhance other resonant qualities. This results in a fuller sound.

Let it be noted that a full sound does not necessarily mean louder or bigger. It means a healthy balance of high, middle and low frequencies. The front nasal resonance provides the high frequencies while enhancing some middle ones. The raising of the soft palate provides the lower frequencies and enhances some middle ones. Too much of the former can result in a strident tone. Too much of the latter can result in a dark and unpleasant tone.

Your soft palate shares a connection with the base of your tongue. When you raise it, the rear of your tongue depresses. Therefore, great care must be taken. If you raise it too far, you create unnecessary tension and muscular force that will detract from your tone and resonance. Over-achieving can reduce the high frequency 'ring' that helps your voice carry, and can make the sound 'muffled' or dark or 'covered' or 'swallowed' or strained. Wherever you create tension in your mouth and throat is where your vocal tone will focus. The soft palate is made of soft and pliable tissue which is not great for reinforcing sound. It is a 'space enhancer' and not a 'sounding board'.

Some styles of singing engage the soft palate a great deal, whereas others do not. The more classical the style, the more soft palate space is needed. That is because the classical genres require not only the bright frontal resonance but also a measure of back resonance. Some singers of pop or rock or country-western or other styles may or may not engage their soft palates at all.

Usually it will enhance your singing to raise it a tiny amount. Also, a general guideline is to drop the base of your tongue to some degree toward the rear wall of your throat for lower pitches, and not raise your soft palate quite so far for higher pitches. This is because your larynx and tongue base will want to rise naturally for higher pitches, especially above your register break, and fighting too hard against what is natural will cause strain.

Common Problems

- Have you ever been told, or even convinced, that you should always sing as if you had an egg or golf ball in the back of your mouth? I disagree with this approach, much to the annoyance of some singing teachers, because the images are too strong. Creating that much space is uncomfortable. It darkens a singer's sound by increasing tension and reducing the flow of breath into the nasal cavities (where the sound's high frequencies or 'shimmer' or 'ring' are enhanced). The singer sounds like he/she is trying too hard with air coming out under varying degrees of pressure, thus making the tone and the lyric flow heavy, deliberate and stilted.

- Pushing the tongue flat with too much force causes tension in the back of your throat. Try it.

- Heavy tension in the rear of the tongue, mostly caused by pressing it down too forcefully, will cause the soft palate to arch too far. It is not easy to lift the soft palate without simultaneously pushing the tongue base down.

- Over-arching the soft palate can cause some singers to push their lips forward too much.

- Pushing the lips forward off the teeth in a forceful and unnatural manner can cause some singers tension in the soft palate and jaw.

- Over-arching the soft palate can cause rigidity in the jaw and the neck.

- A soft palate raised too far can cause outward breath to be strained and placed under too much pressure.

Strategies and Exercises

- There is a fine line between over-arching the soft palate and lifting it subtly. I suggest the following:

  1. First relax your soft palate and sing with it (and thus the rear of your tongue) in a natural resting position.

  2. Get accustomed to that for a few minutes.

  3. Raise it 1 millimetre (or a 16th of an inch), no more. You cannot measure this, obviously. It means it is essentially the smallest movement you can make.

  4. Imagine the soft palate is displaying the tiniest hint of a smirk. This is more of a mental image than a physical action.

  5. Maintain that vague hint of a smirk comfortably and consistently throughout all breaths, pitches and vowels.

  6. Now *allow* your sound to rise through and beyond the soft palate to your face and up into the cavities of your head.

  7. When you sing a more classical style, increase the soft palate smirk sensation to more of a grin, but do not overdo it!

- Consistent space in the rear of your mouth is crucial. Resonating vowel sounds should join as closely to each other as possible by having a rear mouth space that is *very* subtle and always there. For me, a tiny smirk in the soft palate is enough and is the image that works.

- If the image of a smirk in the soft palate does not work for you, try imagining that your soft palate is widening or broadening.

- Some singers aim to sing every word and pitch through the same internal vowel sound. This requires some experimentation to find the vowel or shape that works for you. Read more about this in the chapter on vocal placement. This approach works for some and does not for others. (For my personal set-up, it is too mechanical, muscular, and fatiguing.) You might find your own descriptive image.

- Another way to think of it is that the smirk of your soft palate releases your jaw hinges, as if that smirk were connected and supplying 'oil' to the hinges.

- Sing everything through the beginning hint of a yawn. Go no further than the barest hint or first twitch of a yawn. Do this only after getting the frontal mask resonance firmly in place. Be sure it is the beginning sensation of a yawn and not the end. If you end up yawning through your practice, that is not at all unusual.

- Imagine that your ears are lifting.

- At all times, deal with the tiniest adjustments and increments that you can. It should always feel extraordinarily subtle and unforced.

- Always feel like your outward breath is rising like steam or vapour into your head cavities. Never allow your breath to be placed under heavy pressure nor your vocal sound to focus in the rear of your mouth and back of your throat.

- If a trusted listener tells you that your sound is bigger and more resonant, you may be on to something. If it is not, or if you feel muscular aches and fatigue, certain muscles are working too hard and getting in the way.

For some people, a big smile when singing can cause the larynx to leap up. The same can apply to some people when they sing with the sense of a smirking or broadening soft palate. For others, these approaches work very well. Use what works for you and provides a free, flowing and relaxed tone. There is no cure-all that will help everyone.

Chapter 9

Vocal Placement & Weight

Control and surrender have to be kept in balance. That's what surfers do – take control of the situation, then be carried, then take control. In the last few thousand years, we've become incredibly adept technically. We've treasured the controlling part of ourselves and neglected the surrendering part.

Brian Eno - musician, composer, record producer, singer – in an interview with *The Guardian*, April 2010.

How and where to place or focus the voice is an aspect of singing that can be a complicated challenge for some. It can also be one of the most difficult concepts to explain. The information in this chapter should be interpreted while remaining mindful of earlier information about breathing, the jaw, the tongue, the throat, the epiglottis, the soft palate, and neck tension.

By this stage of this book, it should not surprise you to learn that I favour developing a simple, uncomplicated and natural placement to be the foundation of all your singing.

There are so many subtleties to vocal placement. I do not profess to have all the answers. No singing teacher has. What I can do is express some of the goals for a singer and share some of the approaches that have worked for me and for my students.

Common Problems

- voice feels tense and fatigues rapidly
- muscles of the pharynx, tongue base and throat regularly become tired and sore
- voice produced with heavy pressure and strain

- throaty, pinched placement and swallowed sound
- heavy darkening of the tone, usually from tensing the base of the tongue
- tongue tension and retraction of the tongue
- flatting in pitch
- nasal or thin tone
- over-achieving with space in the pharynx and soft palate
- breath management problems
- inability to sing high and soft – difficulty going into the upper range without pushing with too much breath pressure
- difficulty singing a legato line, due to abrupt changes in breath flow
- vowel distortion
- vibrato problems – too pronounced or too fast or just unstable
- forward thrust of the chin or jaw
- listening to your voice in your head and adjusting to what you like to hear there
- over-singing
- lack of colour variation in the voice
- not knowing how to change

The 'Let It Out' Approach

A full and resonant sound requires a mixture of front and back resonance. The front nasal resonance (the 'mask') provides the higher frequencies in your voice that carry further and provide shimmer and ring. The back resonance provides the 'meatier' lower frequencies to fill out your sound and enrich it further. Too much front resonance can sound strident, thin and harsh. Too much back resonance can sound dark, heavy and even swallowed.

Your best resonance is produced effortlessly. Your best vocal placement is effortless; often deceptively and surprisingly so.

Any pressure or strain will detract from your resonance.

The key to resonance is to **relax**. The goal is energy efficiency: to produce the most powerful and full sound you can with the minimum of effort. It is vital to remove unnecessary strain and rigidity from the muscles of your mouth, tongue, throat, head, face and neck.

Placement is about where you direct the outbound breath that carries sound before it leaves your body. Resonance is simply vibrations that create tone through and within your mouth, throat, and nasal passages.

Placement has a strong effect on the timbre of your voice. Different styles of music, as well as different ensembles, require a variety of placements and timbres. Some of them are dramatically different while others are subtly so. For example, the placement and timbre of an opera singer are very different from those of a pop singer.

A mixture of both front and back placement/resonance is needed for a full vocal sound. How a singer mixes and balances those depends upon his/her skill level and the style of vocal music. Generally, the more classical the style, the more back resonance is added. But just remember that even classical styles use front resonance. Front, or nasal, resonance is natural and something you are born with. Back resonance is learned. Be very careful when you learn to add back resonance that you do not over-achieve and reduce the brilliance of your front resonance. The over-achievement happens most commonly in the forms of tongue tension (the base of the tongue particularly) and soft palate tension.

My approach is first to return to what is natural, become comfortable with it, and then add small amounts of back resonance at a time.

How do you trust this approach? If it is hurting or fatiguing, it is wrong for you. If it is feeling easy, free and painless, you are on a better track for you.

Singing with greater resonance is not about being louder or pushing. It is about using all the resonating spaces and chambers your body has, and using them as effortlessly as possible. The most powerful resonating space you have is above your hard palate and behind your nose. This is the nasal cavity. When your sound accesses this chamber, to you inside your own head it may sound harsh, perhaps even strident. That is not necessarily what others hear. If you tense your tongue and throat, or place your outward breath under heavy pressure, you reduce the sound that can enter this chamber and be enhanced. If you successfully allow the sound to circulate in that behind-the-nose space, your other resonating spaces in the mouth and throat will be free and relaxed to do their job. However, if you concentrate your efforts on the back resonators too much, your sound will focus there and will not have the brilliance you desire.

By the way, do not confuse nasal resonance with singing through your nose. Front, nasal resonance is natural and unlearned. We humans use it as infants. The cry we use from birth is reflexive and requires almost no conscious thought. It has bright high frequency and it carries a considerable distance. An infant can do it for hours without becoming hoarse. Yet an infant has no conscious control or ability to shape vowels or consonants and has no concept of vocalizing words. Everything to do with speech in a person's life is learned through observing and copying. Some people develop a speaking voice that is filled with front resonance – sometimes more than is pleasant – while others develop one with more guttural tones. There are so many factors – family speech patterns, accent, environment, socialization, language spoken, illness, injury, and so on.

Back resonance is learned rather than innate. Done well, it can enhance and enrich the voice. Done unsuitably, it can suppress the natural front resonance.

I recommend you use your natural front resonance as the foundation of your singing and master that before making adjustments. Many singers over-achieve when trying for back resonance. Additionally, I have seen singers taught in a fashion that is detrimental and will cause them years of struggle. In most styles of singing, the forward placement and sensation is paramount to understanding how to stabilize intonation. If back resonance is brought in before forward is understood and habitual, resonant power and 'ring' will be reduced.

Many singers come to lessons and are immediately taught about raising the soft palate and making as large a space as possible. This is a noble endeavour and a skill that a singer should learn. But bear in mind, it is not terribly comfortable and can potentially cause unwanted tension, especially in a novice. A good coach of a novice will start with natural speech and vocal patterns, teach the singer to free those processes and do them as effortlessly as possible, then extend them into singing, and only then begin to add other techniques for enhancing resonance.

(This next part is where some vocal purists would really shoot flames at me.) Allowing outward air through your nose and mouth simultaneously is *sometimes* perfectly acceptable, provided you do not create an unpleasant nasal sound. If the breath is allowed to pass through all the passages of the head, which thus includes the nasal passages and sinuses, that is very natural and comfortable and produces a fuller sound. ('Full' meaning it has a combination of low, mid and high frequencies.) Many purists will say that when you pinch your nose closed while vocalizing there should be no change in the tone. Generally that is appropriate. But, just for example, during my years with Realtime quartet, I had difficulty maintaining a consistent ring in my sound when I sang an 'oo' vowel. It clearly did not have a timbre similar to my other vowels and thus was not placed ideally. I experimented and then demonstrated different ways to my quartet mates. Each time they preferred the sound of my 'oo' vowels when I allowed air through my mouth and nose simultaneously. And they said it was not unpleasant or noticeable that I was doing so. Now, of course, this approach will not be helpful to every singer. Everyone is different. But it shows that the option is available. The balance of how much breath and sound passes through the mouth and nasal cavities can be a challenge. Some voices need to deliberately direct a lot through the nasal cavity, and others not so much. But it is not 'illegal' to do so. For my voice, it is essential to do it if I am to ring an 'oo' vowel. I know of another exceptionally skilled barbershop champion singer who allows air into his nasal passages for his more open vowels like 'ah' and 'oh'.

By now it is clear that the larynx should not dominate a singer's attention, unless, of course, that larynx is not functioning properly. It is the sounds and sensations focused in the mouth, throat and other cavities of the head that determine a singer's effectiveness.

Strategies and Exercises

This is a collection of ideas, strategies and exercises. See, feel and hear what works for you. Some may be helpful, some not. Everyone is different.

After going through these, return to the section about the soft palate. In other words, do these exercises with your soft palate relaxed and become comfortable with them. Then experiment with soft palate adjustments in small increments.

- The key to resonance is to **relax**. If your sound pushes or bursts out, stop and start over. Aim for consistent easy breath flow from start to finish and consistent suppleness in your throat. Keep your tongue loose and relaxed so it lays down 'lazily' for vowel sounds and does not twitch around or retract or bunch up. Release your sound rather than push or force it out. Get yourself out of the way and allow your voice to rediscover its natural resonant power.

- Try singing with a feeling that you are doing nothing. That means allow sound out of you in the easiest way possible. Use no control mechanisms and no muscles to pitch. Just allow sound out and let your voice go where it wants. It can be quite fun to do this.

- Ignore what your voice sounds like inside your own head. It is not how others hear it. It is easy to develop a voice quality inside your head that you like and want to reproduce. But have you ever heard yourself in a recording? You probably were surprised at how different you sounded. You must learn to trust physical sensations and the feedback from trusted people instead of shaping your voice quality to suit your internal hearing.

- Refer back to the sections about the tongue and neck tension.

- Sing notes and lines like they are placed at the roots of your top front teeth and spread out at that level across the width of your face. Imagine you have warm vapour or steam rising gently through the nasal space. This is the 'mask'. Maximum resonance in this space is achieved only when the other muscles relax and get out of the way. Trusting it can require a big paradigm shift but the results are worth it because you can achieve 'energy efficiency' – stronger output and better stamina from less effort.

- Sing notes and lines like they are placed across the bridge of your nose.

- Experiment by singing with breath flowing through your mouth and nose simultaneously. Try it with different vowels. A trusted listener will tell you what sounds pleasant and consistent, and what does not. You may think some of it sounds terribly strident and nasty inside your head, but that trusted listener may have differing views. Keep what works and discard what does not.

- Simply breathing in and out through your mouth and nose simultaneously is an excellent exercise. It can be done properly only when your soft palate, tongue base, pharynx, epiglottis and larynx are free and supple.

- A strong mask resonance should sound a little like glass shattering or should make a piercing, ringing sensation that is focused through your face. Remember it must be effortless and never pressed.

- If you over-achieve with the nasal resonance, there are two simple ways to adjust it:
  - Drop your jaw a little lower. This will allow your throat space to open a little further and mellow the sound without removing the nasal resonance. But drop your jaw only, not the rear of your tongue, and do not retract your jaw toward your neck.
  - Just *think* or *imagine* that breath is flowing through your mouth and nose simultaneously, rather than physically doing it. For some singers, the mental image is enough.

- It *should* be easier to be light and bright with high notes. With low notes, never make them happen or try to make them 'bigger'. Low notes also should flow out naturally. I always tell basses not to prove they are basses, which means no pressing the notes out and no growling sounds. Bring the light and bright sensations of higher notes into your lower register.

- Lip trill to songs. i.e. Bubbling. Do this as much as you like at any time of day or night. Never clench your teeth.

- Sing entire lines/songs and alternate back and forth between lip trilling and singing the words. At various moments of lip trilling, simply drop our jaw open to the word. Do nothing other than let it fall open. Remember how it feels immediately after dropping open from the lip trill. That easy and forward tone is the way to go. But watch that you do not 'retreat' from it back to old habits.

- When you encounter tightness and strain for higher notes and upward intervals, lip trill into those notes and then drop your jaw open to the vowel. Your voice should be naturally and ideally placed. It is easy, however, to retreat very quickly from that sensation when you drop your jaw and to revert to controlling muscle habits. You do not need those muscles or straining efforts to sustain or control your higher notes. Far from it. When you drop open from the lip trilling, the immediate physical sensation you should feel is very, very easy. Sometimes surprisingly so.

- Breathe consistently and freely through high notes and soft notes, just like you do through other notes. Otherwise your resonance could collapse and tension could increase.

- For upward intervals, keep the breath flowing through them and think of them as effortless and remaining in the same placement. When making a leap up in pitch, it is easy to momentarily halt or slow the breath flow because you are preparing to 'place' the higher note. Keep the breath and tone flowing to the end of the lower note and allow the higher note to join onto it. There is no need to 'reach' or 'place'. Keep your breath flowing consistently through the interval. Even if you are asked to separate the two notes, still use the breath as a connector. An excellent exercise is to practice the phrase 'Somewhere over the rainbow'. The octave leap on 'somewhere' is a good test of your tone flow and breath flow. Repeat it in different keys.

- Allow your sound to focus in front of your teeth, especially on high notes. But try it for entire lines, regardless of pitch or vowel.

- Allow higher notes to drift further forward in your face and in front of your teeth. Beware of flattening your tongue, even slightly. Don't do it.

- Sing while gently holding or touching your septum with your thumb and forefinger. (The septum is the flesh separating your nostrils.) Do not block your nostrils. Memorize that sensation and approach, then reproduce it without holding the septum. Keep the throat muscles relaxed and supple at all times.

- Let your head flop forward until your chin is resting on your chest. Do not support your head at all. Keep your torso comfortably upright. Sing in that position. (Your jaw will work more than usual so your head bounces a little on your chest. That is normal for this exercise.) In this position it is difficult to engage or tense your throat muscles and the base of your tongue. Good. Make a note of where the resonant sensations happen. Remember the physical feeling of that placement and replicate it easily when you raise your head again.

- Bend down like you will touch your toes, but bend and release your knees. Let your arms hang loosely from their sockets with your fingers on the floor or on your toes. Do not support your head or neck or shoulders at all. Let them hang completely loose. Sing in this position. (It will be difficult to breathe fully. This is normal. Do not be concerned.) Feel where the physical sensations occur when you sing. Replicate those easily when you return to standing.

- Sing notes, lines and even entire songs replacing each syllable with 'ning'. Sing onto the 'ng' so that the vowel is very short. For the 'ng', have your tongue make contact with the roof of your mouth as far forward as possible. Aim for the hard palate rather than the soft palate. Make the short 'i' vowel zing in front of your teeth with strong nasal power. Use normal breath flow; do not push or explode the breath. You may feel the placement and resonance around the roots of your upper teeth or you may feel it buzzing your nose.

- Hum without vibrating your lips. Stay relaxed and with a heavy jaw. Where does this place your voice? Now try singing 'ng' with your lips lightly closed. Now try humming in a way that tickles and vibrates your lips. Whichever feels the most effortless for you, sing in that same placement.

- As you sing with a heavy and dropped jaw, add a slight lift to your cheeks, from the corners of your mouth to your ears. Make it only a very slight lift that is just enough to give your face a vaguely pleasant expression. Feel wide as well as tall in your sound. Keep your jaw, tongue, etc relaxed.

- Many singers have been instructed for years to sing 'tall' vowel sounds. That is they should either create or imagine a mouth and throat space that is very tall in shape. This is good for creating a warmer, rounder sound. But try adding a sense of *width* to that. In some vocal genres, width is a very unused and underrated quality. A combination of tall and wide can be stellar.

- Imagine your nasal cavity is inflated or filled with buoyant helium.

- Imagine your sound emerging effortlessly from your entire head in all directions. One way to imagine this is to think of a piece of uranium emitting its radiation. The radiation flows consistently, evenly and continuously in every direction. Let your sound fill all the spaces of your head and radiate outward in every direction.

- Imagine you are a frill-necked lizard with its neck skin fully expanded. Stay relaxed while using such a mental image. Being Australian, I grew up seeing such lizards regularly in the back yard. But some readers may not know about such a lizard. Therefore, a photo is included to demonstrate.

- Allow a gentle stream of air to rise into your sinuses like steam or vapour, whereupon it becomes a whirlwind inside those sinus cavities.

- For higher notes, think of your soft palate feeling wide and broad. Allow your breath to stay flowing so as not to shy away backwards from them.

- For lower notes, first bring the sensations of higher resonance to those notes. Next, drop the base of your tongue a tiny amount. Just tiny. You should find a better resonance. But do not press the tongue down too far or you will feel and hear a less pleasant quality.

- Not every vowel sound needs the exact same space between your tongue and the roof of your mouth. But every vowel needs a *sense* or *mental image* of consistent and easy space. When you sing with the most natural voice at your disposal, you should be able to see in a mirror plenty of front surface area of your tongue. A relaxed tongue is not flat like a table, but has a convex curve all the way to the tip. Be very wary of flattening the tongue or dropping it down or bunching it. Tiny adjustments may occur, but dramatic changes are a danger sign. Experiment with the resonant sensations with each vowel sound, so that you have the same experience and placement with each. You may even find that the strongest resonance on some vowels occurs when you do not drop the back of your tongue as far as you have been doing habitually. For example, I once sang my 'ee' vowels with deliberate internal mouth space. However, I sounded covered, dark, muddy and forced. Now my tongue surface area is easy to see, my jaw is loose, the sides of my tongue may even lightly touch the insides of my first molars, and the space between my tongue and the roof of my mouth was much narrower than I had previously thought allowable. (Yes, I am aware I just repeated something from an earlier section.)

- Ensure that the shortest notes and syllables have a pitch and tone to them, especially in rhythmically challenging music. The legato line of flowing tone includes those very short notes. It is disruptive and less exciting if there is no note on them. That does not mean every syllable needs to be sounded in a deliberate or heavy or unnatural way, rather that the tonal flow of the line be paramount. Try singing these well known lines of lyrics and consider the pitch of the syllables marked in italics:

He's *the* boogie-woogie bugle boy *of* Company B.

Oh, I heard *it* through the grapevine.

Do you hear *the* people sing, singing *the* songs of angry men?

- When considering the above comments, an argument can be made for shortening syllables and notes in some cases, for stylistic reasons or for effect or simply because it is more natural. Consider singing the first line of *Polly, Put The Kettle On* with the 'u' in 'put' extended. It may sound a little odd to do that. Most times it will need to be shortened a little to provide the kind of rhythmic separation that is closer to how we would speak it and to make it more appealing to a young child.

- When in doubt, or if your habitual mental processes are so entrenched, open your mind and go natural. For example, sing while doing the hand circle exercise mentioned in the chapter "It's All Mental".

Other important considerations

> *Glottal stops and starts are forbidden, unless for deliberate effect that is crucial to the performance. The disruptions to your breath flow, freedom and resonance can be awful.*

Personal note: Sometimes I practise the ideas in the previous section more deliberately and to a greater degree than I would need in performance. For example, I rehearse and warm-up my front resonance to very unpleasant levels at times. Still free and unforced, but stridently unpleasant. I will not perform with such extreme technique, but the principles will always apply. If I rehearse going too far, I can always adjust back a little. If I never go far enough, it is impossible to produce it for a performance.

Some singers and teachers will encourage a way of forming vowel sounds that involves pushing the lips forward into a rounded position off the teeth. This can be vaguely reminiscent of the bell shape at the end of a brass instrument or can be a variation of the embouchure that brass instrumentalists make with their lips. If required to do this when singing, it is important not to over-achieve. A little rounding and shaping of the lips can be helpful to vowel sounds such as 'oo', 'er', and 'oh'. Opinions are mixed about whether to round the lips forward for an 'ee' vowel sound. Personally, I do not for 'ee', unless conveying a specific attitude or expression, such as pouting or trying to create a darker and more dramatic timbre. Thrusting the lips too far out from the teeth will place strain on the tongue, jaw and larynx, thus darkening and 'covering' the sound and reducing nasal resonance. Having said all this, for some individual singers this lip shaping can help. Some singers have such strong nasal resonance naturally that a little rounding and mellowing of their tone may be more pleasant for the audience. I have seen and heard very mixed results. Most often, however, I see over-achieving and heavy tension, not to mention some ridiculous facial expressions. What works for one singer does not always work for every singer. What is important is to experiment and have a trusted ear tell you what is optimal for *you* – free, unforced, clean, resonant, ringing, and *consistent*.

Once you have found the resonance that works best for you, set the resonant space/alignment and sing everything through that. Do not try to place and resonate each word or note individually. Practise every song by singing everything through the same placement and sensation. Aim for a consistent, clean sound and resonance throughout entire lines. Your diction and articulation should not interfere with your vocal placement and should not add weight or pressure to your sound. Refer to the chapter about the tongue and articulation.

Do not allow word transitions to interfere with your resonance and placement. Mastering this requires a high level of skill and self-awareness. It is very easy for the articulation of a word sound, particularly a consonant, to interfere with the resonance that precedes it and follows it. As mentioned earlier, articulation must be done nimbly at the front of your mouth using the tip of your tongue, your teeth, and your lips. Why? So that your jaw, throat space and rear part of your tongue can remain free and your sound can remain consistent and flowing. If you allow your resonant space to close, even a little, for the transitions from syllable to syllable, you break up the flow of your vocal tone and break up the musical line. Not only should you breathe consistently and effortlessly through word transitions, but you should keep the resonant space and alignment consistent without them becoming static or rigid.

A man who also sang in an International Champion quartet once showed me, when he coached my quartet, how he sings everything through an internal 'er' shape. He sets that idea of a vowel shape inside his mouth and keeps that image through an entire line of music and lyrics. While 'er' did not work comfortably or naturally for me, I began to understand the importance of a consistent space or shape. I tried other internal vowel shapes during that coaching session. There was a distinct improvement in how our quartet kept our sound ringing right through lines without being disrupted by word transitions. However, I was also experiencing some fatigue in the muscles of my tongue and throat, which told me I was using those muscles too much. When our quartet next rehearsed, we tried to reproduce what had been achieved in that coaching session, because it had been exciting and we knew it was important to our continued improvement. But we could not reproduce it successfully, or at least consistently, and spent an hour becoming frustrated. When we cleared our minds and suggested that we return to the way we had been singing before the coaching and add only a *hint* of what our coach wanted, suddenly magic happened. Our sound had effortless ring that flowed without stopping. It even felt like our breaths were ringing and resonant, because we were breathing through that same easy space. We never looked back and won the International Championship later that year. It was in that moment that two important factors became clear to me:

1. **Find *your* way of doing what the coach wants.** I realized this when I analyzed what I was doing to create that consistent space. The only way I could describe what I was doing with my soft palate is to say it felt like it was displaying a hint of a smirk.

2. Sometimes reproducing exactly what the coach wants is not the way to go. Instead, aim to **incorporate a hint of what the coach asked for into your own personal way of doing things**. The adjustment does not have to change you. There may be a way to fit it into what you already do.

Keep on the journey of allowing the forward nasal resonance to do its thing. Trust that to provide the strongest power and overtones in your voice. Master that and then add back resonance in tiny increments, so that you maintain supple throat muscles at all times. Always finish a phrase with the same suppleness as you begin it.

Do not adjust your resonance when you sing with the aid of a microphone, unless you are aiming for a particular effect. You should sing with the same energy, placement and projection as you would without the microphone.

Be Flexible and Adaptable

Most of the exercises and strategies you have just read involve sensations of lightness and ease in the vocal production. They should not involve weighty or heavy effort. Good resonant singing should feel light and effortless. Occasionally increasing the vocal weight can be appropriate for special effects and dramatic moments, but you should return immediately to the easy foundation.

In general, too much vocal weight is unhealthy and can cause a variety of vocal problems. Too much weight in higher pitches is never healthy for your voice. It can result in difficulty reaching those higher notes, tuning problems, a squeezing and straining feeling, unpleasant vocal texture, and a general lack of vocal freedom. Too much vocal weight can make a singer sound heavy and dark, but can also make that singer sound strident and thin. Pop singers often take the full, chest voice higher than usual. In a pop singer with good quality vocal production, this can create an extraordinarily powerful, colourful and dramatic effect. In a pop singer with lesser quality vocal production, it will sound squeezed, nasty and colourless. Singing high notes with vocal weight can be very damaging if pushed too hard.

Some trained lower voices, such as basses, may produce an overly dark sound, often accompanied by pronounced vibrato. This is often due to the base of the tongue pushing the larynx down too forcefully. I used to depress the base of my tongue too much for my lower notes and listened too much to how I sounded inside my own head. I could not achieve full freedom in my higher register until I changed these habits.

Whatever style you may sing, the foundational principles of singing remain the same: no unnecessary tension anywhere!

Choral: When blending with other singers, your placement should remain natural and consistent, but you do not need as much potent resonance or personal volume as you would when singing solo. Also, your vibrato should not be heavily pronounced. It is not possible to match voice timbres appropriately if one member, or more, has a wide vibrato.

Classical: This requires a very full resonant tone, especially opera. These forms of vocal music come from a history of needing to fill large concert halls and theatres, often over an orchestra. This requires significant soft palate space and back resonance, without losing any front nasal resonance. Of course, not all operatic music is created equal, and some operatic works require a lighter vocal quality than some grander ones.

Pop, Rock, R&B, etc: These styles of singing require a great deal of forward nasal resonance. The rear mouth and pharynx space may not be as wide open but should be free of tension and never squeezed.

Country & Western: Singing country music can have some strong similarities to pop music. It doesn't always, but it can. The delivery of country songs can often have clear similarities to delivering speech. Some country speaking accents have a great deal of 'twang', from a certain form of nasal resonance, which give the vocal music a distinctive sound.

Jazz: Jazz singers almost always use a microphone, often sing with instrumental accompaniment, and use very light or intimate vocal resonance. In addition to having a light and free resonant quality, jazz singers use many vocal textures. Nonetheless, they need a clear tone and clean accuracy with pitches.

Musical theatre: This requires strong, sometimes powerful, resonance, although not as powerful as with opera. There are several styles of musical theatre and a variety of amplified and unamplified situations. The Broadway style requires a strong resonance unfortunately nicknamed 'belt'. (Unfortunate because the word can convey a sense of shouting and forcing, which is not at all what good Broadway singers do.) In other forms, the belt would be inappropriate and overbearing, thus the resonance needs to be toned down. Much depends upon the score, the theatre, the orchestra, and the desires of the stage and musical directors. Be flexible and stay true to the essential principle of singing: no tension and no pushing.

Register Break

Singing above your normal vocal register does not need to be difficult; it merely needs to be respected and understood. Pushing too high with your regular 'chest' voice can be tiring, can sometimes sound horribly strained, and can even cause damage. So, then you wonder when and how you should switch into your 'head' voice, also called falsetto. There is an area in the voice of about 3 or 4 semi-tones called the passaggio – the 'no man's land' where you are caught between the two voice registers and have not the same power or control at your disposal.

Ideally, every singer should maintain an even timbre throughout the passaggio, so that the transition from chest voice (usual register) to head voice and back again is not noticeable.

First, and most important, the essential principles in this book still apply. That includes breathing, your jaw, your tongue, your front resonance, and so on.

Some things to notice about singing in head voice:

- Place your finger on your Adam's Apple and sing a note in mid-range of your regular chest register. Then sing a note high in your head voice or falsetto. You will feel your larynx rise. This is natural. Do not try to fight it.

- You will find that when singing in that head voice you will have a narrower space in your epilaryngeal tube. You will also feel that the gap between your tongue and the roof of your mouth is narrower. This also is natural and normal. It is vital that this opening always feel supple and comfortable.

- Sometimes you may think you sound squeaky or like Mickey Mouse or a chipmunk.

You have two goals:

1. to find your most resonant head voice that has colour and does not sound significantly different from your chest voice

2. to develop a mixed voice whereupon you have the option of singing notes in the passaggio with a technique that blends chest and head voice together.

Head Voice / Falsetto

- The feeling or mental image like you have breath flowing out through your nose as well as your mouth is extra important in head voice. With your larynx raised and the epilaryngeal space narrowed, less sound will vibrate in your throat and mouth spaces. This is where the head cavities take over, hence the term 'head voice'.

- It may feel like you are very close to singing through your nose. Do not be afraid of using the nasal resonance in head voice; it gives the voice carrying power. You will know if you are singing through your nose too much. Instead of singing through your nose, I am referring to *breath* through the nasal cavity behind your nose and above your hard palate. Singing through the nose sounds awful, but resonating in the nasal cavity has bright resonance and ring.

- **You must be *flexible* and prepared to *experiment*.** A head voice quality that is wonderful for a classical solo will not be ideal for a close harmony a cappella ensemble, and vice versa. A tiny adjustment can make the tone horribly nasal and thin or can make it too rounded and 'hooty'. There is no one perfect way or method. Use what works for you and serves the music best.

- Try this. Sing an 'ee' vowel at a comfortable head voice pitch. Do it again with your tongue completely relaxed so its sides may even be in loose contact with your most forward molars. The space between your tongue and the roof of your mouth will feel narrow in height yet wide also. That space must also feel free and supple. Sing it again and allow some of your breath to float out through your nose as well as your mouth. The quality of the sound will be thin and nasal, yet also will sound loud in your head considering the lack of breath pressure required. It should feel like everything is happening in the mask area of your face, as if the sound were generated in the cavity behind your nose. Good. Now, as you sing like that, move the back of your tongue downward the tiniest amount, like a millimetre or two. The sound in your head should suddenly 'pop' out much more strongly with a rounder 'hoot' quality that resounds through your mouth. If it does not, try again. It is important to do everything in a manner so subtle that movements and adjustments are no bigger than a millimetre or two. If you leave the rear of your tongue completely relaxed near the roof of your mouth, someone listening to you may say it sounds harsh and nasal or that it sounds excellent and appropriate and free. Every singer is different. If it is harsh and nasal, try moving your jaw open a little further as well as ever-so-subtly dropping the rear of your tongue. As you move your tongue down in this exercise, someone listening may say it sounds beautiful and full or that it sounds too 'hooty' or swallowed (the Mickey Mouse quality). If you move your tongue down too far – and that is easy to do – the vowel will lose its clarity and become indistinct and 'muddy'. **It is vital to experiment with these approaches and these tiny increments. It is astounding how dramatic the difference can be with just a minute adjustment. Every singer is different, yet every singer must discover, memorize and reproduce consistently the alignment and placement that works best for him/her. Being able to adjust from genre to genre is so much easier if you are aware of, and able to control, the miniscule movements that can alter your tone dramatically.**

- As you experiment with the exercises in the paragraph above, if you also experiment with soft palate positions, do so only in the *most* subtle increments and only to find the strongest resonant sensations you can. Do not arch up your soft palate. You do not want to interfere with the ring and ping in the sound. When you sing in your chest voice, often a slight lifting sensation in your soft palate can increase resonant power and improve tonal quality. In your head voice, however, raising your soft palate has potential to interfere, unless you are *highly* skilled. While the chest voice involves a sensation of lifting, the head voice sometimes requires a subtle and gentle opening of the space in a lowering sensation.

- Feel like your sound is going through your hard palate. If it feels like it is going through your septum in this head register, it will sound harsh and thin. If it is focused into the soft palate and mouth too much, you will sound like Mickey Mouse.

- Once you find the ringing sensation in your hard palate and face, you may think your vowels are wider than you are accustomed to and loaded with a 'twangy' quality. As I said before, *experiment* with all the qualities and placements at your disposal. All of them are available to you for a purpose. Make choices based on the music you sing. Have a trusted listener tell you what is free, pleasant, resonant and consistent.

- Once you find the ring in your hard palate and face, ensure the warmest air possible is flowing out of you, without changing the nasal front resonance. It should come out and rise like steam or vapour. Adding that sense of warm air can help balance out any potential harshness or stridency in the tone.

- The vocal weight and pressure must be reduced as you move into your passaggio and head voice. Think of your throat space and the rear of your tongue being wider. Think it, don't muscle it.

- The nasal ring and ping must do the work for you. You cannot muscle head voice at all. You must give up control and take a leap of faith.

- Find your 'wheelhouse' pitches and vowels where your head voice really shines. Any notes below these that are 'hairy' or weak or unstable will require a mixed voice.

- You will run out of breath faster in head voice. This is normal. Accept it.

Strengthening and Stabilizing Your Mixed Voice

As its name implies, your mixed voice employs a combination of some elements of your chest voice with some elements of your head voice. It is a difficult concept to explain. When you reach the passaggio and have not the clarity or strength in your head voice for those notes, take a light vocal quality to your regular chest voice and allow your vowels to spread a little wider in shape. The resonance should feel like it is going ever further into the cavities of your 'mask'. It must be a relatively light production because heavy pressure or belting will most likely result in a horrid wailing tone, or a yelling tone, or a spasm and clunk in your larynx.

Always keep your jaw and tongue loose. Always allow breath to flow evenly, consistently and naturally. The moment you grip or squeeze the breath flow is the moment that mixed voice becomes more challenging.

The 'Cuperto' exercise.

Repeat this exercise regularly to strengthen and clarify your mixed voice.

- Place your lips into a clear 'oo' shape, so that the aperture in your lips is circular. Then create an 'oh' shape behind that inside your mouth. Now siren up and down your entire range, which includes through your register break. Repeat.

- Do this several times a day.

- Do not speed up or slow down your sliding siren. Maintain the same speed throughout. It is common to increase or decrease speed around the passaggio range, due to hesitance.

- Siren through every note. Do not skip any. It is common for singers with an untrained mixed voice for the voice to skip past the passaggio area without singing the notes there. This is the most crucial part of the exercise.

- Your aim is to siren the entire range consistently with seamless, unnoticeable transitions between registers.

- It is normal to initially have some 'clunks', wobbles and unstable areas. Keep doing the siren at the same speed through them and with consistent breath flow.

- You may find that going up is easier or vice versa. Start in the direction that is easier and finish with the direction that has more difficulty.

- Be patient. This can take time. Some singers can make seamless transitions after only a few weeks. Some take considerably longer. Yours truly needed two years.

- After several weeks of this exercise, you will find your mixed voice becoming more comfortable in your music. It will also be more flexible, less fatiguing and filled with head-pinging resonance. Remember that the mixed voice feels 'wider' than chest voice and head voice.

Lastly, it is possible to apply pressure to your mixed voice to produce a long high note. Sometimes it is necessary. It is pretty much the only time a singer may use the epiglottis to place the breath flow under strong pressure, much like letting air slowly out of a tyre. The throat opening will feel wide (horizontally) and the breath flow will be much slower due to the epiglottal pressure valve. However, there are some trade-offs. First, you will fatigue quickly if you repeat it over and over. That can cause damage. Second, you will have difficulty articulating when using that technique, so it is generally for one vowel sound only at a time. Third, you lose flexibility and agility and it is difficult to change pitch. You may be able to move down in pitch, but moving up is more difficult and potentially hazardous. Fourth, pushing too hard risks a 'blow out'. Fifth, you must place vowels differently. They will feel wider and thinner than usual. You must know what notes you can hit in good quality for this technique and not be tempted to go for glory above them. My personal mental pattern when holding a long high note is to think to myself throughout, "Relax… forward… relax… forward…"

Transitioning

You must choose the places in a musical line when you will change from one register to the other. A good singer will follow the same pattern and make transitions at the exact same points every time.

Simply pick the syllable that will allow you easiest access to the new register. Some find it on open vowels like 'ah' and 'oh; others on singable consonants like 'nn' and 'mm' and 'ng'; others still on less open vowels like 'ee', 'oo' and 'er'. If clunking and 'yodeling' persists in a line of music, try a different syllable for making the switch. Whatever is effortless and sounds seamless.

As you transition, think of your soft palette or pharynx space being wide, laterally. It may even help to slightly lift your cheeks and the corners of your mouth as if they were connected to your ears. Whatever happens, keep your breath flowing evenly and allow your mask nasal resonance to do the bulk of the work.

Chapter 10

Practising

Do the things described throughout this book. Many of them can be done at any time of the day or night.

But there is more to practising than mere repetition. To me, the word 'rehearsed' does not mean merely practised over and over. It means explored, developed and refined until:

- I know exactly how I personally belong in the music and the story;

- my true self shines through;

- until the technique is invisible.

The amateur practises until he gets it right.

The professional practises until he cannot get it wrong.

The artist practises until 'right' and 'wrong' have been transcended.

Strategies

Becoming a better singer requires commitment, passion, drive, and discipline. The only source of those qualities is you.

To be a better singer, a few tips and techniques applied once a week at choir rehearsal are not enough. That is a recipe for stagnation. The improving singer may be amateur in status, but must be professional in commitment and drive. The improving singer will commit to continuous improvement, continuous experimentation, continuous feedback, and continuous searching for more freely-produced vocal sound and emotions. Put another way, the improving singer has an open but determined mind all the time.

It is about the physical and mental habits you form, not just the repetition of physical exercises. To accompany the free release of your voice, you must have a determined purpose.

When you learn an important new technique, or make an important improvement, you need to apply it to all your music. This requires the discipline to go back through your music and 'relearn' each piece. As has been discussed earlier, muscle memory and mental patterns become habitual for every piece of music in your repertoire. One moment of executing a new technique will not change the habits already established in all your music. You must rehearse and relearn using the new technique over and over again until there is no chance of old detrimental habits returning. If you do not go through this process, your old and unwanted habits will return at the moment you least desire: in performance. It is when you are under the conditions and pressure of performance that you will find out what is truly habitual. It may seem laborious to relearn every line of music while applying new approaches, but it is part of what a singer does. Are you serious about improving or are you content with an isolated moment of improvement in just one song? Are you content for old habits and patterns to repeat themselves or are you committed to mastering new techniques across your entire repertoire?

Put simply: successful artists are successful because they do what others don't. Sporting people may have said something similar: champions do what others don't.

It is also important to retain perspective and patience. Many of us – me included – can become attached to a new skill that we learn. Sometimes we even become obsessed with it. However helpful or transformational it is, that skill is one cog in a large wheel. It is not the wheel itself. Some people, after years of singing, had to start again by creating a new wheel before adding the cogs one at a time. I had to. I had to establish how to breathe in the easiest way I could and release sound in the easiest way I could, and only then refit other skills to that.

Do your best to work on vocal technique in performance context. Assume you are performing with full emotion every time you open your mouth. Even exercises should be artistic. For example, your inhale is part of the performance. It is not a stop in the action, or else the musical flow will be very disjointed. The speed, duration and nature of your inhale should support the musical and lyrical themes.

Use the 'drop in' breath as inspiration as if you are just thinking of the words and emotions for the first time. Use that breath to pluck up the courage to say the words. Establishing such artistic habits in your technical rehearsing will be of great benefit to you. Sometimes, believe it or not, concentrating on truth, honesty, emotions, and the message of the music will solve many technical problems.

Knowledge plus experience equals wisdom. In the case of a singer, knowledge plus experience plus consistent execution equals freedom to grow. There are good teachers and advice to be found in abundance, but it is up to you to practice, learn, and execute. If you do not practice enough or do not put in the time to retrain your muscle memory to unconsciously execute new techniques, then your improvement will stagnate and your enjoyment will wane.

Students of singing should use the early morning hours and fill their days with the various branches of their study. Sing every day only so much, that on the next day you can practise again, feeling fresh and ready for work, as *regular* study requires. Better one hour every day than ten today and none tomorrow.

The public singer should also do his practicing early in the day, that he may have himself well in hand by evening. How often one feels indisposed in the morning! Any physical reason is sufficient to make singing difficult, or even impossible; it need not be connected necessarily with the vocal organs; in fact, I believe it very rarely is. For this reason, in two hours everything may have changed.

Lilli Lehmann.

Chapter 11

Performing

Choosing Music

> *Choose music to show who you are, not merely what you can do.*

Wait. What has choosing music to do with your performance? You no doubt chose the music ages ago. Now it is time to hit the stage.

When I look at choosing new music is when I first begin to visualize a performance. For me, it is where the performance begins.

Have a vision for music you choose. The more specific the vision you have, the better. Start to picture what you may look like when performing and what the setting may look like. Start imagining the effect it will have on the audience and on you. See the structure of the music and the lyrics as a roadmap to what you want to say in your performance. What is the music saying to you? What are the lyrics saying to you? What can you say and reveal about yourself through the music? Think about both the good and the bad things.

If you are part of an ensemble, if someone has a very clear vision, be sure it is shared with the others. If someone is excited about a vision and has strong ideas about it, trust that. Consider why the song appealed in the first place. The vision is born in your initial gut reaction and emotional response. Your job is to allow the audience to share in the same emotional gut reaction you had.

Be original. You are different from any other singer. Why would you try to imitate another? Do not just copy someone else's performance or choose music only because it is 'cool'. Art needs more than that.

Look at the range in the music and the skill level required. Are you up to it? Be realistic.

Choose and understand the predominant themes of the piece of music. Is it driven by the lyrics? Or by rhythm? Or by emotion? Vocal texture? By drama? Personal experience? Is it primarily about a harmonic fabric of sound? Choose now the theme or themes that you want to pursue and explore.

Be creative. Ask why things must always be done a certain way. There may be different ways to stage a performance. You might take a slow rubato-style ballad and turn it into a quicker song, or vice versa. Consider solos, groups, costuming, character, position on the stage, entrances and exits, and so on.

Approach lyrics like an orator delivering poetry. Look at the lyrics in sections as well as at the key lines. Each section needs a different intent, motivation, even variant of emotion. Nothing should be 'the same' or repeated the same way. Allow yourself to consider physical and facial responses to certain lyrics and lines. Let yourself go in front of a mirror. Use what is fun, satisfying and feels natural. Discard what is forced or contrived.

It is *your* song. It is vital that you can see right now how the music will become yours. Do not merely learn and reproduce the notes and words that somebody else composed. Do not merely reproduce what a musical director says. Even if an ensemble's musical leader sets a vision that is different from yours, you are still free to tell your own personal story through the group's performance plan. Your performance and experience will be much more satisfying.

> **It is not enough to sing the words and the music. You need to know why they need to be sung.**

Identity

> **When you perform, be yourself. You already have the costume.**
>
> **Your best performance and being your true self are inextricably linked.**

Who are you? Really. Truly. Where do you fit into this world? What is your purpose? This is very philosophical for singing, but vital. Every successful singer has known exactly who he/she is. Know who *you* are in every song and every thing.

Are you inspired? Do you know what inspires you? Do you know why? In detail? Do you really know yourself? Warts and all? Do you accept yourself?

Technique is important in singing, but it is nothing without your unfettered passionate inspiration. Remember those. **Unfettered. Passionate. Inspired.** Anything less is selling yourself short.

Performing on stage and being your true self on stage – I am not convinced these are separate concepts. (I know many singers who do separate them.) Find how they join together. Even when playing a very different character, you must show something of your real self if that character is to be believable. An important step in linking together 'performing' and 'being yourself' on stage is to know your performance style. Some people are extroverted and enjoy communicating directly with the audience. Other singers do not enjoy that. The extroverted performer must be careful not to 'play' to the audience too much. It becomes pretending and audiences see through it. (Unless that is the style of show.) If you are an introverted performer, you should not feel pushed into doing an extroverted kind of performance. Internalize the emotions and character instead. Just think about them, feel them, live them, and experience them. For real. Do this for yourself through the music. Stand there and release your feelings with almost no thought of who is watching. Your body and voice will respond. Let yourself go and allow the audience to observe you living and being. Choose the way that is best suited to you and is true to who you are. Let it out.

Phrasing

The core of good musicianship in singing, aside from singing the correct notes and words, is the legato line. More often than not, when the legato line is present in a performance, the audience is moved and touched emotionally.

Earlier sections of this book have discussed delivering a smooth, flowing, uninterrupted stream of sound from vowel to vowel, with just the tip of the tongue gently and nimbly doing most of the articulation. It is more musical than breaking up the sound. Be aware that it is easy to think you have mastered it and are executing it well in your singing until you record yourself and listen later.

Every phrase should have some shape to it, so that there is some rise and fall to the line and a clear direction. Shape a phrase by thinking of releasing your sound, breath and resonance forward as you approach the end. Allow this to happen. Do not manufacture or muscle it. Simply release it and relax it forward through your mask and allow your body to move with that sensation. In fact, do this on all extended notes. It is easy to think you must 'hold' a long note, but this produces physical rigidity and thus a static tone in the line.

Another approach to the end of a phrase or extended note is to think of your jaw falling open a little more and the corners of your mouth rising slightly. Again, allow this to happen in a comfortable and natural way. Your body and stance may even respond naturally.

As you approach the very end of every phrase mentally ask yourself a short question about what you just sang. A question like "Why?" or "What?" or "For what?" or "What's so special about that?" or "Who?". Or think of your own questions. You may even repeat the same question phrase after phrase. Do not allow any phrase to simply end. Asking a question of yourself will connect you to the next phrase and give you a clear reason to sing it. It will also assist you with a concept in phrasing that is often elusive and poorly explained: forward motion. Forward motion is nothing to do with speed or tempo, but is related to how you shape a piece of music and connect the phrases together.

Use different speeds for your inhales between phrases. Be quicker or slower to support the energy or emotion of the moment and to connect to the next line. Be sure you have mastered the art of a simple, unhindered, unimpeded breath through a loose and open space. A loud gasp or heaving chest breath is very distracting.

As has been mentioned already, the inhale is part of the performance as much as the sung music. Use it as the inspiration to find the words, as if they just came to you, or to connect your body to your emotions. As the breath drops into you, drink in the emotions. Even a pause between phrases should be a crucial part of the performance. It should be physically free and connecting naturally between what was just sung and what follows. With a free jaw and a deliberately executed breath that connects with your entire body and leads into the next words, the pause will draw your audience closer to you in anticipation.

Last, do not try to control the music. Let the music control you. Do not sing the music. Let the music sing you.

Energy, Presence & Character

> *There is a world of difference between trying to be exciting and being excited.*
>
> *Performance energy is you being you.*

Energy when you perform has little to do with your bodily movement, or how hard you try, or even choreography. Energy should emanate and radiate from you because you have a clear purpose and a strong vision for your music. Energy should flow from you in continuous waves, even when you are standing still and not singing. One image I like to use is a piece of uranium. Its radioactive energy flows outward in continuous waves, in all directions, and at a constant rate without diminishing. Your energy flow should not resemble the spikes and drops of a heart monitor. Think what that would do to your singing.

Once you have made relaxed, flowing singing and breathing a habit, you are free to allow your performance energy to come out. Do not push it out or pulse it out. There is a world of difference between trying to be exciting and being excited. Your open, free jaw and throat help you connect with your centre of gravity and centre of emotion.

Here are some other tips and approaches I use regularly:

- Do not attempt to 'own' the stage. A true performer *belongs* to it and is one with it.

- Wherever you focus your eyes, fill the room with your resonance and presence. Regardless of the size or shape of the space, or even if it is outdoors, let your presence and sound explore every corner, surface and feature in every direction. When you look at one specific point and do this technique, you will have a more powerful presence without effort and you will feel your focus opening rather than narrowing. It also connects to your breathing and stance.

- Let your presence 'wash over' all the other performers on the stage. Even if you cannot see them all, let your presence find them and wash over them. Connect with everyone else and keep washing over continuously. This is an extraordinarily powerful technique to use in an ensemble. The energy and synergy the group feels is remarkable.

- Feel physically comfortable. Discomfort and awkwardness are obvious. Loosen your hips, pelvic muscles, neck muscles and shoulders to enable better flow and glide into your presence and movements.

- When you perform a move or a gesture, finish it and release it deliberately with a flowing or gliding motion. This can be done quickly or slowly to suit the emotion of the moment. It is vital to return and connect with your presence and core. Never just drop or throw away a move or a gesture. That is distracting and throws your energy away.

- Hands. If you need to move them, do *specific* things that support what you are singing. Have a specific intention. Otherwise, if you have nothing to do with your hands, do nothing. Let them stay by your side with your arms hanging heavily from their sockets. This may feel strange to you but is not as strange as standing there with a hand vaguely out at waist level waiting for a coat to be hung on it. That looks awkward and uncertain.

- Be aware of how you use your eyes and where you look. When you look somewhere or at something, have a specific reason for doing so. If you like, allow your eye focus to be the focus of your performance. Guide the audience where you want them to go. Use clear eye focus on important lines and lyrics, especially when you sing the words that are the title of a song. Make a point with your eyes. Picture who or what you are singing about. Or get inside someone's head with your eyes. Seduce with your eyes. Invite with your eyes. Indulge with your eyes. Live with your eyes.

- Sometimes we singers must do character work, just like actors. Do not think this involves 'putting on' a character or 'putting on' a performance. That is merely pretending and imitating, which comes across as fake. Instead, look for a piece of yourself in the character and a piece of the character in yourself. This is what (good) actors do. Focus on what the story is all about. Be specific about who you are, what the music is about, and whom you are addressing. When you must be a character, just *be* it. Do not try to project it. Be the character, don't play the character.

- Explore your choices. Try different scenarios and emotions for expressing the same song. Each mood or scenario you choose will have a profound effect on your physical performance as well as on your vocal resonance and texture. For example, sing a piece of music as if you are desperate. Then sing it like you are ecstatic. Then try longing and yearning, pleading and begging, despairing, at a wedding, at a funeral, holding a newborn baby, and so on. The only limit to your choices is your imagination.

- The performance begins before you walk onto the stage. Get your thought patterns, presence, energy and physical state ready backstage because the moment you enter you will set the mood for the audience. It is much harder to go through this process after you enter the stage, although you can enhance what you began backstage.

What you think about, the audience will think about

If you feel nervous, your audience will notice it and feel nervous about your performance. If you are general in your thoughts about your music, your audience will give you a general reaction. If you feel awkward in your stance or presence, your audience cannot relax totally and accept your performance openly. If you are under-prepared, your audience will judge the performance from that perspective. If you are hoping or trying to get it right, your audience will be hoping that also. If you are overbearing, over-confident or getting in people's faces, the audience will react accordingly. If you become self-conscious about a mistake, your audience will focus on that mistake.

Conversely, if you are open and honest, your audience will recognize that and accept your performance better. If you are clear and specific with your vision and plan for the music, the audience will be clear and specific in its reactions and experience. If you are vulnerable in your emotional story-telling, your audience will be free to be vulnerable and transported into their own personal emotions.

And so on. You get the idea.

You must be unafraid to make a mistake or to fail. Lose all your inhibitions and doubts, or else they will always hold you back. If you trust your emotions and experiences in your real life, then trust them in your performance. Only by taking some level of personal risk will you achieve your goals. A safe performance will be unsatisfying.

Release all your expectations. Just live in the moment. Take care of the present moment and the outcome will take care of itself.

It is **your** show. Do not ask for anyone to like it or you. Do not expect anyone to like it or you. Give your performance with truth, courage and abandon. The audience will reflect what you give and who you are.

If you sing in an ensemble, love every second on stage with each other. After all, performing is a special privilege. It is easy to get caught up in the technical goals and forget the simple joy of singing. If you want your audience to love you and everything you do, love each other and everything you do together.

Personal experience

Channel your real-life and personal experiences into your singing, even when playing a character. Those experiences are part of the growth of you and help to make you unique. You are not compelled to interpret words literally. Let the musical and lyrical climaxes take you back to a real event in your life. You possibly had that response the very first time you heard the music you are about to perform. Three of the songs that Realtime quartet sang in its International Championship performances touched me on a deeply personal level and had done so from the first time we looked at them in rehearsal. The songs and lyrics did not necessarily make *literal* sense to me and my life's experiences, but the *tone* and emotions sure did. When singing them, I was channeling real and personal stuff.

If you are not reliving personal experiences when you sing each piece of music, or projecting the things you have always wanted to be, why are you singing in the first place? Singing is an art, and art is inspired and created by individual passion.

Get your personal stories clear and specific. If you are taking on a character, be very specific. When you know the exact details, the audience will have clarity.

Follow a pathway that is natural to you and never suppress who you are in your regular life. If you regularly have bizarre or humorous thoughts (I sure do) then allow those during your singing, because you will look like you instead of a 'performer'. If you do not usually show emotion in life, I can guarantee that you *have* those emotions and that you *feel* them as strongly as anyone else. Allow your personal feelings and unique thought patterns to colour your voice in a variety of ways, and to accent important words, while always maintaining easy and consistent air flow.

Caress specific words using a sensory approach. You experience everything in the world through your five senses, so use the memories of how things look, feel, taste, smell and hear to colour the key words. Sometimes you might have a combination of senses. For example, if the word 'kiss' is in the lyrics, remember that a kiss involves not only touch but also taste and even smell (the smell of the other person's skin, perfume, hair, breath, etc).

The Fourth Wall

This concept has been known a long time, but I pay tribute to Conrad Keil for explaining it to me so well.

In a traditional theatre with a proscenium arch and a three-walled box set, the fourth wall is an imaginary wall at the front of the stage between the audience and the performers. The audience observes the action of a show through that imaginary wall. The actors in a play traditionally interact with each other and do not play directly to the audience. If an actor delivers an aside to the audience, this is known as breaking the fourth wall. Even speaking directly to the audience through a camera in a film or television program is considered breaking the wall. A soliloquy, where the audience observes a character delivering an inner monologue (e.g. Hamlet's famous "To be or not to be" speech), is delivered from behind the fourth wall. The audience has no involvement in the soliloquy other than observing it.

How the fourth wall is used is a decision for the performer or director. A song can be delivered in:

1. **presentational** mode – fourth wall has been removed and the performance is communicated directly to the audience

2. **representational** mode – the fourth wall is in place and the music and message is delivered entirely behind the wall to person(s) not present but imagined, or as a soliloquy, or even to other performers

3. **combination** – the fourth wall can be in place for parts of the song and then broken during other sections.

All of these options can help give a song greater dramatic scope, while the third option can also provide variety to a long piece of music.

The fourth wall is a mental concept only. Thus its advantages and limitations are determined entirely by a performer's imagination. A performer may break the wall at any time and may also go behind it at any time. Moments for doing this should be chosen wisely so as to support the themes of the performance and the music.

When preparing a performance, a singer should consider the following questions.

1. Who am I for this piece of music?

   - Am I me?
   - Am I playing a character?

2. Where am I?

   - In a specific place indicated by the stage set?
   - In a personal setting inside my head?
   - In a setting I want to convey to the audience through my costume or props or gestures or demeanour?
   - Is it an intimate or public setting in my mind?
   - If I am in an imaginary setting, what am I looking at?

3. Who am I talking to?

   - Myself?
   - Another person?
   - The audience?
   - The world or the universe generally?
   - About another person?

4. After answering questions 1-3, will I be in presentational or representational mode?

5. What am I really saying in this music and with these lyrics?

   - What is the subtext?

- Does the emotional theme relate to my personal experiences?

6. Why am I singing and saying this?

    - What is my motivation or reason?

    - Should it be delivered as if I am starting a new thought or conversation, or should it be like a reaction to something already in progress?

    - Why would anyone think to express these things?

7. Can the fourth wall change during the music? Are there moments when I can go behind the wall? Are there moments when I might break/shift the wall and shift my role?

8. Does this approach fit with my ensemble and its approach?

Unless you are very skilled in stagecraft, it is best to work through these concepts with another person who can observe what has impact and makes sense and what does not. For example, it can have great impact on an audience and on your performance if you choose to 'punch' through the wall at a key moment or on key lyrics in the music.

When you perform behind the fourth wall, the sky is the limit in your mind. It is a safe place for you. It may be just like a special location in your house or another place where you rehearse difficult speeches that you want to say to others. In such a safe environment, ask what personal and truthful side of yourself you are determined to show the audience.

In addition, behind the wall is a different way of performing because you can draw the audience toward you, rather than sending energy directly at them. For some, it is a big shift in thinking, but it can have a powerful effect. There are many reasons to choose to be behind the wall: safety, being alone with personal thoughts, reliving memories, pretending like you are 'jamming' with a band, communicating with other performers, and any other reasons you can come up with.

Last, consider how holding sheet music during the performance affects you, your audience, and your vision for the music. If the music is exceedingly complex, then it is quite appropriate. Otherwise, can you gain better rapport, involvement and dramatic effect with your audience if you take the stage without the sheet music? Just like with the fourth wall, the choice is yours.

Nerves

Feeling nervous before a performance is normal and human. Some singers may feel it only slightly, while others may experience pronounced anxiety and strong physiological reactions. Others still may have an experience somewhere between those extremes. Everyone is different. It is partly a mental game and partly a physiological one.

The 'fight or flight' response is a physiological response to something that is perceived as threatening or scary. This is when your heart beats faster, adrenaline starts pumping, your breathing becomes more rapid and shallow, you feel butterflies in your stomach, your hands and knees may tremble a little, you feel the need to go to the toilet frequently, you may begin sweating even in cool conditions, and several other possible reactions. This is your body doing what it must to protect and preserve crucial organs and functions. It also affects your focus and can make you much less aware of your surroundings or in your peripheral vision. These are not the only things that occur, but they are quite common for performers.

For a singer, the 'fight or flight' response is a double-edged sword. It can provide a burst of energy and strength to your muscles to make you feel powerful and excited. However, it can also cause physical tension and a lack of freedom and control over your breathing and vocal production. I personally have experienced a strong 'fight or flight' response on a couple of occasions when singing and it resulted in loss of awareness, some quavering in my voice, and a problem called breath stacking, where I could breathe only in my chest, I felt like I could not exhale fully, and thus each inhale stacked more breath on top of what was already inside me. I felt tight and inflated across my chest, which reduced vocal support and spread tension to other areas of my body. Perhaps you have experienced this, also. It is quite common. It also happens often when a performer is keyed up and tries or pushes too hard.

Experience is a factor that can reduce nervousness and anxiety considerably. Being nervous can be related to feeling uncertain about what will happen next or feeling like you have little control over the situation. That is a very common way for an inexperienced performer to think and feel. An experienced singer has been through these feelings before, knows that the situation is very much in hand, and has developed strategies for retaining control and focus. Some experienced singers even know how to use the nervous energy and adrenaline to their advantage by channeling them positively into their performance.

An experienced performer also knows that being under-prepared virtually guarantees feeling nervous.

It is appropriate and normal to feel some level of nerves before a performance. It simply means that you are human and that the moment matters.

Performance anxiety, however, is a more severe problem and is rooted in mental patterns. Severe performance anxiety, where one becomes a nervous wreck or has severe loss of awareness, is more likely to be caused by deeper psychological patterns or fears.

It is important for you to repeat positive affirmations in a bid to boost confidence and lose fear. (See the next section about belief.) These affirmations should be words of encouragement and inspiration that can be repeated again and again, not only before a performance but in all the weeks or months of preparation and rehearsal. It is important to lose all fear of failure, mistakes and embarrassment. What you repeat to yourself and believe is what will be. Therefore, if you have been told negative things for years by a significant other, those things will affect your mindset, especially under performance pressure. If you have grown up feeling pressure to be a quality performer because of your parents, there can be debilitating fear of failure or of letting them down by not living up to expectations. If you tell yourself that you are nervous, you will continue to be and will likely get worse. Use positive messages and cues.

Remember, what you think about is what the audience will think about.

Of course, there are pharmaceutical drugs available that can reduce symptoms of pre-performance nerves. The most common ones are often called Beta Blockers, so called because they inhibit the body's beta receptors and weaken the effect of stress hormones. If you investigate these, please consult your doctor. These medications are available only with a prescription and are not to be trifled with. They were designed for treating medical conditions, particularly heart disorders, nervous conditions, and hypertension. While fellow performers you trust may offer advice and tips, nothing beats professional medical knowledge and advice. They are not sedatives but should help a person feel more normal instead of nervous. Not everyone responds to them the same way, and some can be harmful to people with certain existing conditions, so it is important to seek qualified medical advice. If you do go down that pathway, try any new medication for the first time on a day when there is no performance. You do not want to find out on performance day that a medication is unsuitable or causes an adverse reaction.

Before a performance, do not use alcohol or illegal drugs or other social/recreational drugs. *Ever*.

Belief

As was touched upon in the previous section, your mind plays a hugely important role in how you prepare and how you perform. It also plays an important role in how you process things after a performance.

Here are some random thoughts about belief and being mentally prepared for a performance:

- Release all your expectations. Give your all. Expect nothing.

- Remember the most simple and basic reason why you sing.

- You have nothing to prove. You have everything to share and live.

- Leave your ego at the door.

- Create affirmations to repeat to yourself from your rehearsals and personal practice right through to backstage.

Repeat them and repeat them. What you repeat will become what you believe. What you believe is what can happen.

- You must have unshakeable belief in yourself. That comes not from your ego, but from being one hundred percent content with who you are, in your life, at this moment in time. It comes from being content in every aspect of your life - personal, spiritual, family, relationships, friendships, work, etc. You do not have to be happy with everything. The word is *content*. Accepting. You must accept that everything is as it is and not try to change anything right now. Trying to change or disguise or repress things about you before a performance is a recipe for internal conflict and anxiety. Accept that everything that has happened up to this moment is the only thing that could have happened.

- All that matters is this moment. Right now. Forget everything else. The moment of now is everlasting. Do what you must do right now and do not think about what has happened or what lies ahead. Take care of the moment and the outcome will take care of itself.

- Visualize your performance in advance. During the final weeks of preparation and rehearsal, start picturing the performance space and your place in it. A good time to do this is when going to sleep. Picture everything in your mind – the stage, the lights, the auditorium, the audience, the backstage personnel, the people on stage around you, your costume, the orchestra or instrumentalists, everything. Run through your complete performance silently in your head and visualize it being perfect, successful and effortless.

- Do not try to own the stage. Belong to it. Be part of it. Be one with it.

- Be realistic. Be honest. There is quite a difference between believing something will happen and fooling yourself.

- Know your strengths and your limitations. Accept them. You are who you are. It is what it is. Play to your strengths and avoid or minimize your weaknesses.

- When performance time arrives, the excitement of the moment can make you want to give more 'oomph' than you might have in rehearsal. Doing this, however, means you have become focused on *trying* to *make* your performance exciting, rather than simply *being* exciting. Focus your mind on your own personal power and your own personal story to tell through the music. Channel your adrenaline into maintaining a smooth flow of sound through a consistent, easy space. Focus on allowing your presence to fill the room. If you are well prepared, you *can* focus your being on these things. Live and be yourself. The audience will make up its own mind and does not need to be told how to think.

- There is a difference between body language that is *trying* to sell or convince and body language that *is* *sold* and *convincing*. What you may think is your best energetic self for performance is often different from what actually is your best. Experiment in your own time to find how you can be energetic without being tense - face lit up and expressive, body moving fluidly, breath consistent, eye focus clear, gestures clear. Video yourself and observe.

- Do your best and forget the rest.

Recording

Recording can be a big challenge for a singer, whether it be a studio recording or just recording one's self during rehearsal. Once again, the game is mental. It is easy to get caught in a thought process of 'I must do this perfectly'. This is a noble goal, but it is one that causes tension and a very technical performance. Tell the story, release the emotion, relive the experience, and let it be real to you. There should be no difference in your mind between a stage performance and a recording performance. It is a big mental challenge to do this when recording, but I will take an emotionally truthful recording that has a couple of technical flaws over a flawless technical recording that lacks emotion, colour, texture or truth.

For studio recording, if you can possibly have a trusted advisor there with you, do it. The right person can free you as an artist by helping make the technical process easier, keeping you focused on the task at hand, keeping you relaxed, and bringing out the best in you.

Chapter 12

Talking

Talk in the same way as you sing. Follow the same processes and principles as outlined in this book. Use the same freedom, the same breathing, and the same placement.

Speak in a comfortable middle pitch range. It is easy to fall into the trap of speaking too low in pitch, perhaps believing it is more authoritative or commanding. Speaking too low will wear and fatigue your voice.

Some people talk a lot during the course of a regular day, others not so much. If you talk a lot in your daily work, be careful not to 'growl' when doing so. It does not have to be a loud and harsh growl. Just a low-volume and throaty placement that grates or rubs your vocal folds will be deadly to your vocal stamina.

Do your best to avoid talking above loud noise or to fill large spaces. If you must do it, use very forward nasal resonance for carrying power. Just as when you sing, there should be no strain and no pressure.

Chapter 13

Choosing A Voice Teacher

Critics, judges, family, friends, colleagues, observers and fans can be excellent at pointing out where you can improve. Very few can show you *how*. That is where a good teacher or coach comes in.

There are many excellent voice coaches out there. But how do you choose one for you? With all his/her knowledge, skill and achievements, does the coach follow a set and rigid formula? Or does he/she work with the characteristics of each singer to draw out and enhance each one's uniqueness? I have seen teachers almost ruin some voices by preaching a formula without considering and respecting the individual singer's unique set up. Which will you choose - one who builds a voice on an assembly line, or one who refines a voice based on its unique natural shape? Like the piece of marble that is sculpted and carved into a statue, the statue was always there before the pieces were cleared away.

There are three crucial considerations when choosing a voice teacher:

1. someone who speaks your 'language',
2. someone who will develop your voice in its best and most natural way, and
3. someone who will help you express your true self through your voice.

There are more considerations than these but they make a good summary.

Beware of those who tell you there is only one way of singing – or one genre – that matters. There are 'rules' in some vocal styles about how to produce the voice. It is important that both teacher and student know which rules apply to only one style and which are universal. Keep your mind open. Even a singing teacher who has a closed mind, or who follows only one vocal model, or who points you in the wrong direction for you, can still teach you things. Learn what helps you and avoid advice that encourages you to close your mind. A rigid mindset that clings to a 'pure' set of rules will reduce your vocal flexibility and adaptability, and could cause you to miss out on opportunities to shine in a variety of genres.

Also beware of slick marketers who make big promises. There are no guarantees. A flashy web site filled with jargon and graphics is no indication of the skill of a teacher. Some are genuinely interested in helping a fellow singer achieve his/her best. Some may care about repeat income more than a student's success.

I would hope that your singing teacher will be supportive of your musical choices. For example, some singers I know who enjoy barbershop harmony (as I do) have had singing teachers who actively frowned upon the genre for its music and its vocal production, as if it were unworthy or harmful. While the teacher may be highly qualified, skilled and esteemed, some level of respect for the student's choices and activities is warranted. I believe a teacher should help a student to achieve his/her goals and work *with* the student to find the appropriate teaching approaches and learning styles. Years ago I was delighted to hear Graeme Morton, who wrote this book's foreword, say to our classically-oriented church choir (for which he conducted and also played pipe organ) that he admired the legato line of the barbershop style and thought it an excellent example to all choral ensembles. Good singing and good musicianship can be found in every vocal genre, if we look for it.

It is common for a voice student to accept everything the teacher says as 'gospel' and do as asked. This is fair enough. After all, the teacher is more knowledgeable and more experienced. But do these attributes necessarily make a good teacher? Just because a sporting hero was superb as a player does not guarantee his/her success as a coach. A brilliant actor does not always make a brilliant director. A highly competent employee may not necessarily make a competent manager or trainer.

Let it be noted now that the paragraph above does not grant permission to ignore anything challenging that a teacher asks of you. It simply means that teachers are of mixed abilities, as are students. Some will be particularly helpful to you, some not so helpful. Know this: you can learn something from every teacher.

In my twenties, I took a few voice lessons from some very fine singers who were also lovely people. Either I didn't listen very well or they were not very good instructors – probably the former – but I never really grasped what they were on about or why. I seemed to just do exercises and technique work, while some even encouraged me to enter Eisteddfods singing music I did not like at all. Over the following years, I improved a little, but developed and enhanced some bad habits. Now I can see with hindsight that I learned a great deal from everyone who ever taught me or gave me advice. Even anyone who put me on the 'wrong' track has been an invaluable resource because I began to recognize what didn't work for me. From there I began to see what *did* work for me. Since then, I have delved deeper, looking for ways to do it better.

One thing I noticed about many singing teachers was that they taught technique and little else. Very few would discuss staging, emotional truth, personal identity, why we do what we do, how we express our inner selves and passions through performance, or how to make a piece of music my own. I was fortunate enough to explore these concepts while studying Drama and preparing roles with directors of plays and musicals. As a 'late bloomer', it was years until I began to wonder why singing teachers did not integrate all these concepts together with vocal technique. Even as I majored in English, Speech and Drama in my Bachelor of Education degree, under the tutelage of some exceptional artists, I still followed the path of many university students: I made notes and regurgitated information to suit the lecturer or examiner, without critical thought and without putting my soul into it. I realized that most of my performances had been studies in reproducing carefully learned lines, moves and cues. (I dreaded, and cringed at, the word 'polished' being used to describe my performances.) When creating a work of art, that will never do.

After university, I worked with yet more artists and performing groups, and I came across a variety of approaches to singing. Some approaches were experimental, some were socially oriented, while others were very regimented and steeped in the rigid teachings of one or two teachers. Above all, I learned there is no 'one size fits all' approach to singing. There is no 'one true way', even though in my twenties some of my peers considered classical singing as the only way and any other type of genre as lesser.

It is to be expected that some teachers will follow and use the approaches that are familiar to them. This is natural. This also explains why some are open to different singing genres and others are not. Human beings tend to follow familiar patterns and behaviours. When I was young and brash and egotistical, I unfairly regarded many singing teachers around me as no good. I understand now that they were following approaches that were familiar to them, using the knowledge they had acquired, and were trying to instruct in the best way they knew how. In fact, I learned some things from those teachers, although I could have learned more perhaps. What I needed at that time was a singing teacher who could set my voice free and help me sing music suitable to my voice type and suitable to my personality and style as a performer. Finding that teacher is an important part of a singer's journey.

When you are choosing a singing teacher, I hope you find someone who sets your voice, mind and soul free. I hope you find someone who respects you as an artist who will create new culture rather than merely copying what already exists.

Chapter 14

Young Voices

Great care must be taken with the voices of children and adolescents. Overworking these voices can cause problems that last a long time, sometimes for life. All the approaches and exercises in this book can be applied to young voices. Setting the habits of vocal freedom early in life will serve a singer well as he/she matures.

As a boy I sang each week in a formal church choir. We often sang challenging works. I was fortunate to have no vocal problems during my childhood, but have seen boys in rigorous choral programs develop nodules on their vocal folds by age ten or so. I am convinced this is due to overwork, excessive demands upon the young singers, and an approach to singing that is not healthy for young voices.

It is important not to overwork the adolescent voice, also. During puberty and the teenage years, the body and the voice are not fully matured. The voice especially is not mature enough, settled enough or hardy enough for excessive work. It should be nurtured and kept healthy into a singer's twenties and beyond. Both male and female singers do not reach peak vocal maturity until their thirties, perhaps in the twenties for some.

The adolescent male's voice needs particular care. During the period that a boy's voice is breaking, singing should be reduced or even stopped temporarily. The change from a child's register to an adult's register can take months or years to settle. During early adolescence, the larynx, and indeed the entire body, undergoes rapid and dramatic change. When a young male finds his voice 'clunking' between registers, any singing he does must be gentle. It is vital not to make him sing in his childhood register for too long and equally vital not to push him into a lower register for which he is not yet ready. Some younger singers are encouraged to sing dramatic music at too young an age, which costs many of them their career potential. I was fortunate not to develop vocal problems myself. At sixteen, I played the tenor lead role of Frederic in my school's production of *The Pirates of Penzance*. That role is challenging enough for a mature singer. At sixteen I was simply lucky to have a naturally strong vocal set up and to not damage anything. It had to be luck because my vocal technique was poor and strained back then. Even now in my early forties, I look at the role of Frederic as a taxing vocal challenge.

Overworking a young voice can cause not only physical problems but enthusiasm problems also. Foster the joy of music and help the young singer to experience a manageable level of success. Then you may have a devotee for life. Push too hard and the young singer may become discouraged, frustrated, and ultimately give up singing.

Chapter 15

Ensemble Singing

When you sing with a group of people, you learn how to subsume yourself into a group consciousness because a cappella singing is all about the immersion of the self into the community. That's one of the great feelings - to stop being me for a little while and to become us. That way lies empathy, the great social virtue.

Brian Eno - musician, composer, record producer, singer. NPR's *Weekend Edition Sunday*, November 23, 2008.

Ensemble singing. How do we do it better? Simple. Remember that it is about the entire group working and sounding like a unit. Your individual actions should support the entire group.

Avoid the temptation to sing louder or to put your 'signature' into the group's sound. Submit your sound inside the unit. Ensemble singing can be done very successfully using the same approaches described in this book. Simply allow your sound to be released freely and with artistic sensitivity. You do not necessarily need to hear yourself at all times, either. The unit sound will be bigger when voices lock together and reinforce each other, not when individual voices push and stick out. The more you relax and simply *allow* sound out of yourself with no tension and no muscling (and thus what feels like no 'controlling'), the better your voice will fit into an ensemble. Try it.

Give up control for the sake of the team and simply enjoy the ride with each other. Your director or leader will thank you for it.

Support the style of the ensemble

Singers must assume different roles appropriate to the genre(s) the ensemble sings. Nonetheless, the same principles in this book apply because every ensemble singer needs to be free, flexible and adaptable. After all, someone singing with a country-western style of production in a classical chorale will either stand out or else will adversely affect the consonance of the entire group's output. That singer must adapt for the good of the group and the performance. Similarly, an opera singer using full operatic technique and vibrato within a barbershop harmony chorus or jazz quartet will stand out obviously. Adapting and being flexible does not necessarily mean singing with a fundamentally different technique or compromising your voice. It is about accepting that there are some adjustments to make in a bid to support the ensemble's goals. I repeat what I just said: The more you relax and simply *allow* sound out of yourself with no tension and no muscling (and thus what feels like no 'controlling'), the better your voice will fit into an ensemble.

When in doubt, leave your fear or ego or pride behind and ask for advice.

Vision and goals

What is the ensemble's purpose? Why is it there? What should it bring to its audiences? What does it plan to achieve over the next year? What does it plan to achieve over the next five years?

It is quite easy for an ensemble to have some agreed and stated goals. However, two problems can arise: (1) the group does not take 'ownership' of the goals and (2) the group may not be united in its approach to achieving and enhancing those goals. The leader, or leadership team, needs to ensure the entire group has a say in those goals – and thus ownership of them – and keep everyone focused on those goals week after week, month after month.

The musical director or leader should also have a clear vision for the group. Without a vision, an ensemble risks drifting aimlessly. The vision can cover larger issues like the group's overall identity right through to the smaller details such as the processes for learning new music. A director needs to share his/her vision with the singers. The membership needs to see in clear detail where the director plans to go with the music and how to get there.

In many amateur ensembles, there are some members who strive for increasing excellence and others who are there more for the friendships and social benefits. There is bound to be several people there for both reasons. If you are a member of an ensemble, I urge you always to keep the goals and vision in mind in everything you do. Also, communicate with your leadership team and ask them regularly about goals and vision. Personal goals and ambitions are good to have, but it is easy to become too narrowly focused on those and lose perspective. Everything you sing and do should be to support the ensemble, and as free from ego as possible.

If every member and leader is committed to the same goals and is positive, supportive and nurturing to others, then your ensemble has a good chance of achieving its goals.

Last, but not least, know your notes and words. That may seem an unnecessary thing to say, but achieving goals will be impossible without doing it. Not being absolutely secure with notes and words is disrespectful and is a disservice to the ensemble. Do not believe that you can hide and just coast along for the ride. Do not rely on others to do the work for you. When you sing solo, you always know your notes and words. Singing in an ensemble should be no different.

Identity

For an ensemble to do well, it must know its identity. Who it is, as one body. Its personality.

A clear identity is one of the biggest keys to successful performing. A group that knows who it is will have clear purpose in everything it does.

Identity is about what sets the ensemble apart from others. It can be derived from the group's strengths or things it does very well. When looking to define an identity, look to the group's outstanding qualities. Or look to its role in the community.

The group always sings too loud!

Does your chorus/choir sing most of the time in a volume range of seventy percent to one hundred percent? In other words, do the soft volume moments in the music seem to be fleeting and the group resumes its customary volume level almost immediately? It may just be that many members think they need to hear themselves all the time. Trying to hear themselves is a natural impulse, but it is a 'security blanket' line of thought. As soon as one sings louder to hear himself and be sure he is doing things correctly, another cannot hear himself as well, and thus also sings louder. One by one, this can spread to others. Very quickly, the group is singing at its customary or default volume level. I have even seen many singers become upset and admit being so because they cannot hear themselves in the group.

If you are in a larger ensemble (such as forty or more voices), is it really necessary for you to hear yourself at all times? Is that the only way you can know if you are doing things right? Place your sound inside the ensemble and be happy with that. Allow your voice to be an internal part of the whole. It is about the entire group, not just one voice. Trust that you are doing things right if you cannot hear yourself. (Sing it wrong, even softly, and you *will* hear yourself.) Trying to hear yourself can make your voice stick out, at least to the people around you, if not to the entire audience and the director. It risks the ensemble oversinging and having an unbalanced sound.

There are circumstances where you will inevitably and unavoidably hear yourself singing. These include when the group does manage to sing very softly and when singing in a small ensemble. Also, if you are in an exposed position of a large choir – such as the back row or the end of a row – you have little choice but to hear yourself. However, you get the idea. Serve the group as sensitively and musically as you can.

I must include a special comment about the previous three paragraphs. When I have explained this concept to choral groups, occasionally some members have misinterpreted it as being asked to just sing softly. However, that is not the same concept and they are not the words I said.

Standing next to a poor singer

Do you get frustrated by the person singing poorly next to you? Do you sing a little louder in an effort to show that person how it should be done and get him/her on track? Guess what? You singing louder will not help. Instead, it will make things worse. What can happen is that you stick out of the sound or that others will start to sing louder. You may even be unwittingly covering for that poor singer. Sing your own way inside the unit and allow the person singing badly to be exposed, identified and (we hope) helped.

It can also be frustrating if you are standing next to a 'leaner'. That is someone who has difficulty singing his/her part without the comfort of a stronger singer alongside. There are different types of leaner. One type genuinely wants to improve but has difficulty and thus needs the security of a better singer. Another type may know he/she is not a strong singer but craves the social capital and sense of belonging provided by being a member of the group. Another type still may be someone who simply puts in less effort. There may be many reasons why a singer is a leaner. Whatever the case, unless you personally and proactively provide extra help and support for that person outside rehearsal times, it is usually best to stay out of it and let it be a private matter between the singer and the musical leadership. Remember to leave your ego and frustrations out of the equation so you can do what is best and most supportive for the entire group.

How much rehearsal?

Are you a 'once a week' ensemble singer? In other words, does your personal rehearsing consist only of the singing you do at weekly ensemble practice? Singing at rehearsals, gigs, or recording sessions is not practice. If the group has an agreed goal to improve continuously, but your personal practice is done only at the weekly rehearsal, are you really helping the group improve? Take time to sing and rehearse by yourself without pressure. Take chances, try new things, make mistakes, learn from them, set new habits, reinvent your mental approach, and set goals.

Retaining what we learn

Does your ensemble make great progress when it works with a coach and then within one or two weeks regresses to its old ways? This can be very frustrating. Those who retain the learning become exasperated when others do not. This causes the group's improvement to slow or stop, and can even cause abler singers to leave in search of something else.

There is no magic bullet to solve this problem. It requires detailed follow-up week after week and every member must *want* to do it. Sometimes it is a matter of individual responsibility, while other times it is a matter of catering to a variety of learning styles and speeds within the group.

Furthermore, if reverting to old ways has been a repetitive pattern over a period of years, that is a clear sign the culture of the group needs to be changed in a positive manner. There is a chance that some members are stuck in the 'comfort zone'.

The two key elements are:

- Leadership figures must remind members regularly and effectively of the new learning and techniques. Clear and helpful communication is important.

- Every member, including the leaders, must have ownership of, and commitment to, the ensemble's goals.

Strategies and Exercises for Ensemble Singing

- Maintain a loose throat.
- Drop the jaw hinges open at every opportunity.
- Keep the base (rear half) of your tongue relaxed.
- 'Drop in' inhale.
- Consistent breath flow through every line.
- No over-shaping with your tongue.
- Do what will make your director's job easier.
- Flowing, legato lines.

- Form consonants gently at the front of your mouth. Brush the consonants so you can maintain breath flow. If the director asks for more clipped or articulated consonants, find a way to do it so your breath flow is disrupted the least.

- Feel like your entire head is open and has air and sound flowing through it.

- To help balance the group sound, sing some notes and lines in unison. If your voice is louder than others', reduce your volume (not your breath flow) to fit inside the unit.

- Ensure unison sections in the music are not louder than the harmony sections, unless the composer or director asks for it.

- Maintain some level of body movement, even by millimetres. When you become static, so will your singing and music.

- In a cappella groups, do not try to be synchronized by 'waiting' for each other. All members should assume some sense of leadership and use their bodies and gestures to indicate where the key moments are and where to attack and release.

- When not singing the words but still vocalizing, keep allowing your body and sound to go with the ebb and flow of the lyrics and themes.

- Even when not singing at all, allow yourself to be a supportive and active part of the performance, as if you still are singing. Be in the moment.

- Directors: occasionally conduct with your hands less and simply perform the music more. Allow yourself to be the focus of telling the story and releasing the vision. If you occasionally direct like a singer performing the music, your singers may find greater freedom and scope.

- Ensemble singers, be mindful of becoming complacent or too comfortable. Being part of the group is a privilege that you earn. It is not a right. You should be certain to earn your place in the group with every piece of music. An attitude that believes passing an audition once is an automatic pass forever is dangerous, unhelpful, and a recipe for personal stagnation. It does not matter how good you are, or how good

165

you think you are, you are not indispensable to the ensemble. Leave your ego at the door and bring instead your humility, your passion, your dedication, your discipline, and your desire to serve.

Strategies for group presence and energy

- Be aware of the proximity and energy of all the other singers. Feel like one entity, connected.

- Imagine your presence 'washing' over every other singer. Even though your eye focus may be on the director or on a certain point, keep washing over every other singer. Let that sensation be continuous through the music. When everyone does this, the effect can be very powerful – physically, vocally, and emotionally.

- Allow your sound and presence to fill the room or space. With your eye focus on the director, allow your presence to explore the entire space - forward, behind, sides, corners, up, down, everywhere.

- Maintain the 'washing' and 'filling' presence during tender and vulnerable emotional moments, even during silence or between songs.

- You must feel 100% content within yourself, like nothing can ever hurt you.

- Expect nothing. Give everything. You have nothing to prove and nobody to please. But you do have something to say and give.

- Has the group considered the fourth wall? Ask yourselves for every piece of music – Who are you? Where are you? Set the character and scene as specifically as possible.

How do we grow our membership?

First, you must know your identity. Clearly. Specifically. You must be on board with it. Clarity in your group's purpose will show in performances. That, in turn, is attractive to other singers.

Second, sing better and perform better. In this day and age, the best way to grow membership is to improve the singing and performance level. People these days are accustomed to music being presented professionally, energetically and skillfully. Increased numbers and enthusiasm in your audiences will translate into increased numbers of singers wanting to join. Always strive to raise the group's skill level and do so keeping the group's identity and vision clearly in mind.

Third, always strive to reinvent and challenge yourselves. You may have heard the adage that goes along the lines of 'if you keep doing what you've always done, you get what you've always got'. Improving to new levels involves a change of mindset from the entire ensemble. It is not up to directors or coaches alone. Directors lead the way, while coaches provide help, ideas, and techniques. Each individual singer must be open to the challenge of doing things differently and better. A warning sign can be when members become accustomed to a regular pattern at meetings and rehearsals. Doing the exact same things each week can be comforting and secure for the group, but just watch that the comfort zone does not become too comfortable. Look to the mindsets of each member. Are there some who enjoy the improvements brought about by hard work and coaching, yet still slip back to old habits the following week? Which members are giving and which are waiting for inspiration? It can require a complete paradigm shift for the members of an ensemble to focus on each week as a new challenge, each rendition of a song as a new story, and each performance as a chance to grow.

Fourth, evangelize. Think outwardly.

- Your group is its own advertisement. Step back and look at it regularly as if you were new to it. What do you see?

- Have key people keep bringing the entire group back to an outward focus. It is important to serve the existing members and nurture their development and happiness, but it is equally important to look outwardly and remember that music is art. It is a gift. Share it. Give it. Talk about it. Ensure the music and fellowship are focused on others.

- Have a recruitment process or system.

- Invite people to join. And *follow them up*. Do not wait to see if new people will come along or will return after one visit? Do not just give out a business card and wait. Get *their* business cards and numbers. Call them to make connections and friendships. You do not merely attract members. You attract singers. You attract friends. You attract their gifts and talents.

- Give new people and visitors a special moment during rehearsal. Then keep communicating with them throughout the session. Have a member or two make connections and start to build one-on-one relationships with the visitors while showing them personally what the group is all about and how it works.

- Individual members are the ones who recruit new members. Equip them and prepare them as such. Marketing serves a purpose in generating interest, but it is the one-on-one connections that make or break the deal.

- Perform in your community in a variety of shows and venues. Be in front of different audiences as regularly as practical or possible.

- After performing, connect with your audience. Make this part of your recruitment system. Have materials and information ready. You never know how many new fans and members will come from those moments.

Last, ask other groups what they do and how. You are not alone. Share with other groups and learn from them.

Chapter 16

Vibrato

I have deliberately avoided discussing vibrato until this point. There is a chance that some questions you had about it may have been answered indirectly already.

Vibrato is a regular pulsating fluctuation in pitch. It is used to add warmth and expressive qualities to the voice as well as to instruments. String players use vibrato a great deal and to wonderful effect.

Vocal vibrato can occur in almost any style of vocal production. It can be a sign of skill or of problems. It also increases naturally with age. Vibrato that is done well is a subtle learned technique that can be 'switched' on or off, or modified, as necessary. Vocal vibrato that is not done well is a sign of technical problems and may cause damage over the long term.

Do not confuse vibrato with tremolo. Tremolo is a trembling or even shuddering effect used mostly by instrumentalists, but it can be done by some vocalists.

People's opinions about vibrato are mixed, due mostly to their experiences with it. Some love it and consider it an essential colouring to the vocal tone. Others hate it and consider it a technical fault or just interference in a stream of pure tone. Others still have opinions somewhere between those extremes. Singing teachers particularly can have strong opinions about vibrato. Each teacher has grounding and expertise in a particular genre or two, but it is to be hoped that those teachers will be open, sensitive and adaptable to other genres.

There is a time and a place to use vibrato. Equally, there is a time and a place not to use it. Some music may benefit from vibrato while other music may not. Please respect the music you are singing. Sticking resolutely to one vocal production technique is not always the best way to serve the music. An artist will be flexible, adaptable, and will leave the ego at the door.

A slight vibrato in the human voice is natural and can add colour and warmth to the tone. As a singer ages, vibrato in the voice will increase naturally. Sometimes a singer is trained to create a very pronounced vibrato with a wide pitch variation or a rapid variation, or both. Opera employs a wide vibrato that is more or less present from the beginning of a note through to its completion. In other styles, the vibrato may start later in a note or phrase to round it off. Some styles, such as a cappella harmony singing and certain choral ensembles, require vibrato to be reduced to ensure purity in each voice's pitch so it may harmonize and 'lock' with other voices. There are some forms, such as the music of Palestrina, that require 'straight tone', which is a pure and steady stream of sound. If you listen to The Tallis Scholars sing the music of Thomas Tallis, you will hear an ideal example of straight tone without vibrato.

Some singing teachers will say that straight tone is bad for the voice, even damaging. This is not necessarily the case because there is a difference between producing a free straight tone and trying to suppress vibrato. The latter is a recipe for tension and for a static, lifeless line of music. Keeping vibrato minimized can be achieved through free vocal production, but suppressing it is an unhealthy thought pattern that increases the likelihood of muscular rigidity. Singing without vibrato can be totally natural and free.

Trying to over-produce vibrato is also a pathway to tension and even vocal damage. Some inexperienced or untrained singers have attempted to produce vibrato by manipulating pitch up and down, mistakenly thinking that oscillating the breath flow and larynx is how to do it.

Vibrato is a result of specific vocal technique and most of it will happen automatically when applying that technique as freely as possible. Equally, certain techniques will reduce vibrato naturally without the need for muscular suppression. Making vibrato happen or making it stop will sound strained and will cause damage.

It must be noted that, throughout history, vibrato's popularity has fluctuated wildly. It still does. At various points of the past five centuries, sung music in some parts of Europe employed no vibrato while the fashion of music in other parts required lots of it. Music and its fashions changed over the years as composers created and developed new genres and variations of them.

The 'Let It Out' Approach

This will not surprise you. That's right: let it out. But I do not mean just the vibrato. I mean let your voice out naturally. *Allow* vibrato to happen or not to happen, as necessary. When done well, particular vocal stylings and technique will automatically produce vibrato, while others will not.

Following the approach in this book will generally result in minimal vibrato, yet should also allow some to occur naturally as shape and colour near the ends of phrases and extended vowels.

However, every voice is different. Every person is different. Some approaches will give one singer greater vibrato and another less. **Use what works for your voice type and is sensitive to the music.**

Coming from a mixed background of singing genres, I see the benefits of all approaches, if they are done well. Considering my barbershop experience, most of my singing these days involves less vibrato and more straight tone. In any ensemble singing, the goal is to blend the voices together so that they lock together, reinforce the sound waves, and expand the overtones. Less pronounced (or narrower) vibrato equals more overtone.

Vibrato that is produced well is essentially a breath technique. There are different ways to produce it and they will produce different effects. Opera singers use it partly for breath efficiency.

Generally, the greater the diaphragmatic pressure, and the more the pharynx is opened in compensation to reduce glottal pressure (by raising the soft palate and lowering the base of the tongue), the wider the vibrato will be. In this situation, vibrato is more likely to start immediately on a note and continue throughout. It will convey grandness and breadth to a vocal tone, as well as colour. In many trained singers, vibrato comes from a breath support technique where the abdominal muscles and the diaphragm oppose or resist each other. To sing like this, it is vital that you receive proper training and know what you are doing.

If breath flow is light and free through a relaxed epilaryngeal tube and pharynx, the vibrato that can occur conveys a sense of intimacy and vulnerability, as well as colour. However, there is a fine line here between a squeezed tone and a free tone. The squeezed tone and vibrato will be thin and unstable, thus placing strain on the larynx. Singing an extended note lightly and freely, with an almost airy tone, should generally have little or no vibrato, but a tiny increase in the rate of breath flow (without changing the tongue and throat) should facilitate a little vibrato. Reducing the air flow in such a situation may produce some vibrato, but is likely to be unstable and thin, and also may cause the resonance to collapse and the larynx to partially block the sound flow.

Then there is vibrato for pop singing. While there are many pop singers with good, even excellent, technique, I am generally not a fan of the vibrato produced by the majority in their higher chest registers. It is a double-edged sword because the vibrato in a pop singer's voice is important for shape and colour, but unfortunately so many of them push up to such high notes in their chest registers that the vibrato is strained and under pressure. It can sometimes seem like there is more demand in pop music for vocal pyrotechnics and less for simplicity. When you see a pop singer's jaw shaking in time with the vibrato, it is likely that there is strain and pressure on the entire vocal set-up. While those high notes may be moving and filled with drama and passion, it should be clear which of those singers can expect to have healthy voices for a long time and which can expect problems sooner rather than later.

I implore you to research every piece of music to see if vibrato is stylistically suitable, or not suitable, and how much is appropriate. Look to the vocal stylings of the time when the music was written. Of course, some music and some performances will allow you artistic freedom to go your own way and even break new ground. However, it can be annoying to hear a piece from a specific period in history sung by a voice that has been trained in a manner unsuitable to the musical style. For example, I have heard soloists sing operatic arias with pure straight tone, while I have also heard operatic soloists using heavy tone and wide vibrato for music from the Renaissance. Both were considerably distracting. More modern music often allows more flexibility for the singer to choose. Please research and respect the music.

Be sensitive to the stylistic demands of all forms of music. Baroque, pop, country-western, lieder, Gregorian chant, chamber music, jazz, barbershop, folk music, opera, yodelling, Tibetan throat singing, the list goes on...

A true artist will be flexible, adaptable, and will leave the ego at the door.

Strategies

- **The purpose of this book is to help you set a foundation of free and natural vocalizing, so that any exercises and training you undertake can build upon that foundation. Therefore, follow the approaches and exercises in this book. Allow vibrato to happen or not to happen. Experiment with what increases your vibrato's range or frequency. Experiment with what produces a straight tone for you. Be sure you always stay free in all the key areas where tension can occur. The difference between producing vibrato and producing no vibrato is subtle.**

- **Everyone is different.** When some singers use vibrato, their breath flow is very gentle. Others have more vibrato with a more focused channel or 'column' of breath. Some find that straight tone uses more air, while others find that vibrato uses more. Conversely, some use vibrato as a means of preserving breath and extending it, while others achieve the same through straight tone.

- If you are aiming for straight tone, or something along those lines, avoid thinking like you must sing without vibrato or that it should be suppressed. These are negative thoughts. Use positive approaches and ideas to produce the desired effect. Think about singing right on the pitch with purity, focus and physical freedom.

- Some singers and teachers regard singing with straight tone as singing lightly. That is not necessarily so. Straight tone can be light. It can also be every bit as full, powerful and dramatic as a tone loaded with vibrato. Equally, vibrato can be effective in lyrical singing. The differences are stylistic as well as technical.

- Focus on allowing a continuous and consistent *flow* of breath through every line and note of your singing. Most times, this will reduce vibrato, but not always. Slight increases in the flow rate may produce the vibrato you want. Go back through the breathing strategies and exercises described in earlier chapters.

- Always think of your breath flow as consistent and sustained, rather than held. Do not push on your abdominal muscles nor suck them in. Keep your torso upright and free throughout.

- Keep your neck and jaw free at all times. Straight tone produced with tension in the neck and jaw will be a lifeless, static, stiff, and sometimes unpleasant tone. Vibrato that emerges through neck and jaw tension will be unpleasant because the tightness will flow into your larynx and make it unstable.

- When singing in head voice (falsetto), a tone free of vibrato is quite easy to achieve, while pronounced vibrato is difficult and at times unnatural.

- Listen to as much different sung music as you can. Immerse yourself in different styles that you may not have considered much before. Listen to chant music, English choirs, opera, light opera, vocal jazz, high level barbershop quartets and choruses, Broadway, swing, big band, pop, rock, country-western, folk, Baroque, Gospel, spiritual, sacred, and so on.

Choral and Ensemble Singing

Obviously, for choral and ensemble singing, reduced vibrato is the way to go. The aim is to achieve such blend in the voices that they sound like one voice multiplied. Individual voices that are steady yet free produce stronger overtones – the very high pitched notes that can be heard above the note a person is singing. (Singing is not a science, as I have said, but you can easily research the acoustic science and mathematics that explain this phenomenon.) Groups of voices that match and blend will reinforce, enhance and expand these overtones so that the output from the whole sounds greater than the sum of its parts. It is possible for a group to sound double its size without any voice pushing. Doing this requires clean intonation and diction. Vibrato disrupts and obscures the 'ring' or expansion of the group sound. Singers should be trained and encouraged to align their timbres, resonance and vowel sounds to create a blended, full group tone.

Don't be a hero in your ensemble. You should avoid the temptation to put your personal 'signature' into the sound or to sing louder to help someone near you. Refer to the chapter about ensemble singing for some strategies. Vibrato reduces the chance for the group to achieve lock and harmonic expansion. Be sensitive and adaptable to the genre, the musical form, the situation, the setting, size of the group, and so on. A good singer is always adaptable.

Rehearse regularly singing lines in unison. Aim to sound like one voice reinforced several times over. Any disruption to the lock, unity and expansion will be obvious.

Ensemble singing demands clean attacks and releases, whereas solo singing allows more flexibility. Sing cleanly on to the vowel sounds in your ensemble. The vowel should fall where the note starts (except for when you deliberately sound singable consonants). That means the first consonant of a word needs to be fractionally before it and articulated lightly and nimbly. Singing with a wide vibrato can cause singers to be late with attacks, or at least 'feel' their way into vowels. Doing this in an ensemble can have a dragging effect on tempo and rhythm.

Sometimes in harmony singing, less volume in your part can produce greater expansion and ring. Not always, sometimes. What this is referring to is balance. A harmony section that dominates the others will cause the group sound to be unbalanced and less expanded.

At all times, remember it is about the entire group, not one singer or section.

Listen to as many singing groups as you can, across all genres. It is impossible not to appreciate, admire, and learn from the skill and virtuosity of truly outstanding groups such as Chanticleer, The Choir of King's College, The King's Singers, The Tallis Scholars, Manhattan Transfer, The Real Group, Pentatonix, The Idea of North, Take 6, The House Jacks, The Westminster Chorus, The Mills Brothers, The Four Freshmen, The Andrews Sisters, Rockapella, The Monteverdi Choir, Naturally 7, and so on almost forever. I cannot name all the great ensembles. Just immerse yourself.

Vibrato Problems

Very wide and wobbling vibrato

An expression has been around for a long time describing a singer's vibrato as wide enough to drive a truck through. Either the singer hasn't enough focus in the tone or the attempt to sing with strong vibrato is being hampered by a lack of diaphragmatic power. Remember that singing with pronounced and wide vibrato is a skill that requires careful training. It involves the muscles of the abdomen and the diaphragm working in constant, not pulsing, opposition to each other. It becomes a problem when the vibrato is so wide that the intended pitch of a note is unclear.

Fixing this problem can be done through simple exercises. One is practising the hissed outward breath suggested in the exercises in the chapter on breathing. Singing full lines of music to a sustained but free 'ng' is also an excellent way to bring focus back into the tone.

Very rapid vibrato

When a vibrato's oscillation is very rapid, it can be a sign of tension at the base of the tongue. As has been explored earlier, the tongue can be the bane of a singer's existence. It must be kept free along its entire length, which includes the parts we cannot see that extend down to the larynx.

Another cause of this rapid vibrato is lack of proper breath support, particularly from chest breathing or from the singer using the epiglottis as a pressure valve for controlling breath flow.

Nerves can also play a significant role here. A strong 'fight or flight' response in the body will cause shallower and more rapid breathing, which is thus less supportive of the entire vocal set up.

Diaphragmatic vibrato

This is where the singer pulses the diaphragm muscles – and thus the breath flow – to create what is simply a 'false' vibrato. Unwanted muscle memory can result from this action, so if this problem is identified, remedial work should be done immediately. Return to exercises involving lip trills and the sustained hiss so that breath flow is consistent.

Laryngeal vibrato

This is probably the most bizarre vibrato problem, and also the most damaging. It happens when a singer deliberately manipulates the pitch up and down, under the mistaken impression that this is how vibrato is created. This creates strain on the larynx and continued over time will cause damage. The singer must sing pitches cleanly and purely, and learn to do so with muscular freedom. The problem areas to be released are most likely to be the base of the tongue and the epiglottis. More breathing exercises that involve a steady breath flow are also in order.

Chapter 17

When You Are Sick

> *Rest and be quiet.*
>
> *Drink clear fluids, especially water.*
>
> *Avoid singing if you can.*

Alas, there is no miracle cure when you are sick. You know that.

You also know that singing is difficult when you are sick, especially when you contract a cold or influenza. When sickness strikes, singing should be avoided. If, however, 'the show must go on', seek advice from a respected voice coach and from a medical professional.

When your immune system discovers invading bacteria or a virus, it manufactures appropriate and specific white blood cells to repel the invasion. This is when you feel most wretched. In that situation, resting because you have little energy is a natural and helpful response to what your body is doing.

Rest your voice. That goes double if you have a sore throat, or if it is painful to swallow, or if you have some degree of laryngitis. Pushing through these conditions can cause long-term problems. Listen to your body. Consider the risk of performing. Is it worth causing months of vocal problems? Maybe the show must go on, but if you damage something, you will not be in some future shows that go on.

Some singers and coaches will recommend drugs and medicines. If they are the kinds of medicines that (1) you would normally take when sick and (2) you can get over the counter, then perhaps those may be appropriate and helpful. Be sure to increase your water intake to counteract any dehydrating effects from cold and 'flu medicines. Heavy congestion is tough to sing through, but so also is a dry mouth and throat. Simple things like Ibuprofen and Paracetamol are fine, *in recommended doses*. Ibuprofen is my preferred over-the-counter medicine when I am sick. It is a non-steroidal anti-inflammatory drug for reducing pain, inflammation and fever. It is sold under brand names like Advil, Motrin, Nurofen, Galprofen, and so on. Paracetamol is also known as Acetaminophen and may be sold under brand names such as Tylenol or Panadol. Do not take a new medicine for the first time on the day of a performance. You must stick to what you know and trust.

Antibiotics are issued only by prescription, so leave that decision to a trusted medical professional. They are for bacterial infections only and are useless against a virus like a cold or 'flu. Also antibiotics will not reduce your symptoms instantly nor make you better instantly.

When laryngitis strikes, you have your worst problem. Laryngitis is a condition where the folds of your larynx become swollen, inflamed and even infected to the point where they cannot vibrate freely. Instead they rub together in a manner that causes more irritation. The singer knows that he/she has no voice, or barely any. Pushing those swollen folds to keep vibrating in such a condition will make the inflammation worse. Some singers may talk about an oral corticosteroid as a miracle treatment. A corticosteroid (not the same as an anabolic steroid) is a powerful drug that can reduce inflammation considerably and temporarily. However, it is a *last resort* option, when you absolutely cannot get out of performing, and *great care* must be taken. It is issued only by a doctor and must never be trifled with. Using a steroid can be downright dangerous for your voice. For a comparison example, if a professional football player has a steroid injection into an injured knee, he might be able to continue playing, but he will not feel when he is causing that knee further damage. The same applies to a singer. An oral steroid may give you your voice back, but you must go easy and still stay quiet as much as possible, because you cannot feel further damage being done to your vocal folds. I have seen singers ruin their voices for months afterward by taking a steroid, feeling good, and carrying on as normal. A steroid is a desperate measure. The singer must still rest the voice as much as possible and be prepared for having no voice at all for up to three days after it wears off. It is best to avoid this option if at all possible. Besides, it needs up to eight hours to take full effect and few singers have quick access to a doctor so close to a performance, so it may not even be possible.

Homeopathic treatments and remedies, such as honey and lemon mixtures, should do you no harm. Some singers I know swear by them when sickness strikes. There are singer's teas that you can buy and they are very good. Otherwise, here is a recipe for making some singer's tea. There are more recipes available on the internet.

Ingredients for Singer's Tea:
- 3 litres of water.
- Fresh ginger root (1 or several to make 15-20cm of length).
- 1 lemon.
- ½ a cup of honey.
- 250ml of apple juice concentrate.
- Cayenne pepper.

Preparation:
- Cut the ginger root(s) into slices about the same width as you would slice carrots.
- Put the ginger slices and water into a saucepan.
- Bring to a boil, then simmer for 40-45 minutes.
- Remove the ginger from the water.
- Add to the water the juice from the lemon, the honey, the apple juice concentrate, and 1/8 of a teaspoon of cayenne pepper. (If you can stand it, increase the amount of cayenne pepper just a tiny amount.)
- Bring the mixture to a simmer.
- Serve hot.

Meanwhile, when you are healthy, do what you can to stay that way. Drink water, sleep well, eat nutritious whole foods, and wash your hands regularly.

Chapter 18

Other Concerns & Questions

Excess saliva and gastric reflux

Although a dry mouth can occur for a nervous performer, it is not uncommon for a singer to develop an excessive amount of saliva in the mouth when singing. This can be uncomfortable, or at least disconcerting, because the singer has a strong urge to swallow but may not find a break in the music to do so. If this happens regularly to you, it is worth consulting your doctor about gastric reflux. It is not necessarily the cause of the excess saliva when singing, but it could be. To have reflux, you do not need to experience strong symptoms such as heartburn or a sour, bitter taste in your mouth. The acid brought up from your stomach by reflux can reach your vocal folds when you are lying down and sleeping. That acid can wreak havoc on those folds. If in doubt, see your doctor, check your diet, and do not eat close to bedtime.

Mucus/Mucous

There is a difference. Mucus is the viscous, slimy mixture secreted by your body to lubricate and protect certain tissue surfaces. Mucous is an adjective and refers to anything about mucus, such as mucous membranes. While mucus is not exactly a pleasant subject to discuss for some people, it is vital to the health of your entire vocal set-up. The folds of your larynx are coated with the stuff.

Sometimes a singer may have excess mucus. This makes it difficult to clear the throat because the mucus on the vocal folds is so thick and heavy. If this happens to you, drink more water and check your diet. A little lemon juice or lime juice in hot or warm water is definitely helpful. Reduce or eliminate eating dairy and wheat products. Also reduce or eliminate consuming coffee, sugary drinks, fizzy soft drinks, and alcohol.

If you suffer continually from post-nasal drip or congestion, you can use a Neti Pot to gently cleanse your nasal passages with lightly salted water.

Another helpful treatment is the Entertainers Secret Throat Spray – and sprays with similar names and ingredients – to help the mucous membranes stay moist and evenly coated. You can buy these on the internet and sometimes from other singers.

Do not clear your throat continually.

Dysphonia and nodules

Dysphonia is the medical term for voice disorders where someone can make sound but with difficulty or dysfunction. Most singers automatically think it means having nodules (also called nodes) on the vocal folds, but that condition is only one of several that fit the category of dysphonia. Laryngitis fits the definition, for instance.

But nodules are what singers really fear. A nodule is a lump of tissue that grows on the vocal folds and reduces their ability to function properly. The singer can end up with reduced pitch range, frequent breaks or 'clunks' during phonation, or even some sustained hoarseness. Nodules are vocal damage, plain and simple. They develop from overuse of the voice or from strenuous vocal activity, even from poor technique. Sometimes, however, even singers who are regarded as having impeccable technique and vocal health can develop nodules.

The only solution is to see a medical specialist and follow precisely a specialized and lengthy course of treatment.

Temporomandibular Joint Disorders

Commonly abbreviated to TMJ or TMD.

These are problems with the jaw, usually the jaw joint and the muscles that control moving it. People with a disorder here may have reduced ability to open the mouth very wide and/or a clicking or popping sensation when opening or closing the mouth. Some even experience pain or difficulty when chewing, a feeling of the upper and lower teeth being out of alignment, a tired or swollen face, and even pain that spreads from the jaw joint into the neck and shoulders. There are other symptoms that can occur, also.

The causes are not entirely clear, but symptoms do tend to arise in people who clench their teeth regularly (especially when sleeping) or who have been injured in that area.

Obviously, discomfort in opening and closing the jaw can be a problem for a singer. If this happens to you, see a medical and/or dental specialist. Treatments are available, including hot/cold packs, dietary changes, medications, mouthpieces worn when sleeping, even laser treatment therapy.

Chapter 19

Secrets

There aren't any.

There are no tricks either. There is only awareness.

Chapter 20

Short 'n' Sweet

Because today we seem to want quick, instant gratification and inspiration.

These are in no particular order.

- ➢ It is better to understand a little than to misunderstand a lot. Keep your approach to singing simple.

- ➢ There is a reason you started singing in the first place. It probably wasn't about winning awards. Rediscover that reason.

- ➢ Do not seek the light. Bring the light. Be the light.

- ➢ There is a difference between wanting to sing and needing to sing.

- ➢ What are some good tips for singing? 1. Sleep. 2. Drink water. 3. Live for it.

- ➢ Singing should be easy, free, natural, relaxed, and fun.

- ➢ Singing should not be forced, tense, pushed, laborious, or painful.

- ➢ Free your mind, free your voice.

- ➢ Free your body, free your voice.

- ➢ Get yourself out of the way.

- ➢ Good singing is about working smarter, not always harder.

- ➢ Goals are to breathe freely and sing freely. Relaxed. Unimpeded. Easy. Free. Consistent.

- ➢ A true performer does not 'own' the stage. A true performer *belongs* to it. A true performer is *one* with it.

- ➢ Good singing is good singing. Regardless of what genre of music you wish to sing, the fundamental principals apply: free, open, easily produced vocal sound.

- There are no tricks or secrets to improved singing. There is only awareness.
- The quest to sing better never ends.
- There is no such thing as instant success.
- Think about the journey, not the destination. Think about the moment, not the outcome.
- Leave your ego at the door.
- Accept your strengths and weaknesses. Feed the strengths. Avoid the weaknesses.
- You cannot do this on your computer or smartphone or tablet. This is real. It takes work and discipline and passion.
- When preparing your music and performance, start with the big picture.
- The art inspires the technique. Not vice versa.
- The passion inspires the preparation. Not vice versa.
- *Sometimes* the goal is not to entertain the audience. The audience's enjoyment may be a by-product of your own enjoyment.
- A little knowledge can sometimes be a dangerous thing.
- It is not enough to sing the notes and words. You need to know why they need to be sung.
- The amateur practises until he gets it right. The professional practises until he cannot get it wrong. The artist practices until 'right' and 'wrong' have been transcended.
- Nothing beats correct notes.
- Nothing but a finished product should be submitted for assessment. There are no rewards for good intentions or promising beginnings.
- Sometimes less is more.
- There is a fine line between hobby and obsession. Remember the people who are most important to you.
- Sing everything as if it is the last time you may ever sing.

- What you think about, the audience will think about.
- If it encourages muscle manipulation or tension, don't do it.
- If it is fatiguing, don't do it.
- Give up the idea of 'controlling' your voice. Allow it to go where it wants.
- Bigger is not always better. The volume myth has an enduring allure.
- Louder does not mean pressing, pushing or straining. Louder means sound being amplified more in your body's resonating chambers.
- Don't sing the music. Let the music sing you.
- Don't control the music and the plan. Let the music and the plan control you.
- Ensemble singers, be mindful of complacency. Being part of the group is a privilege that you earn. It is not a right.
- There is the text and the subtext. Audiences have no defence for the subtext.
- The biggest subtext is the presence you project.
- Question everything. *Why* am I singing soft/loud/etc?
- Vocal freedom allows shape in the lyric and the line. Avoid the 'flatline'.
- Accept compliments and accolades with humility and gratitude.
- Don't copy other singers. They sing how they sing. You must sing how you sing.
- Master your natural resonant vocal sound and you can adapt to other vocal genres more easily.
- By following only one rigid technique, you are likely to find out more about what your voice cannot do rather than what it can.
- Dare to try something different. The only barrier is your mind.
- Incorporate any coaching you receive into who you are and what you do naturally. Work on small details but don't fixate on them.
- Sometimes the harder we try, the worse it gets.

- Know your voice's range. It is what it is. Accept it.

- Trusting your natural voice can be a leap of faith. Yet it can be the foundation of everything you sing.

- Choose music to show who you are, not merely what you can do.

- There are many singing teachers out there. Choose one that speaks your 'language' and adapts to your individual voice and learning style.

- The more you relax and simply *allow* sound out of yourself with no tension and no muscling (and thus what feels like no 'controlling'), the better your voice will fit into an ensemble.

- It is one thing to be inspired. It is another to stay inspired.

- Singing washes away from the soul the dust of everyday life.

- When you perform, be yourself. You already have the costume.

- Your best performance and being your true self are inextricably linked.

- Strive to create new culture rather than reproducing and regurgitating what exists already.

- It isn't necessarily about what you "perform" or "present", but what you create and release.

Bibliography

James, Clive. *May Week Was In June*. London: Pan Books Ltd., 1990.

Lehmann, Lilli. *My Singing Art (Meine Gesangkunst)*. Berlin: 1902. New York: Macmillan, 1902. 3rd Edition, 1924, republished: Mineola, N.Y.: Dover, 1993. Translation: Richard Aldrich.

Sharon, Deke. *In Defense of Imperfection*. Blog entry on www.casa.org: Jan 15, 2013. (www.casa.org/node/16424)

Eight ways to de-clutter your mind

1. Accept what is.
2. Be kind to yourself.
3. Release your fears and guilt.
4. Let go of control.
5. Visualize what is important to you.
6. Focus on your life-force energy.
7. Allow yourself to be vulnerable.
8. Let go of what does not serve or interest you.

How to feel fulfilled as a singer

1. Never compare yourself with others.
2. Measure success by how your singing has enriched your life and how you feel when you create it.
3. Continually drive yourself to learn and grow.
4. Know that art cannot be measured purely in dollars, and will only appreciate in value.
5. Trust that when you are making the world more beautiful, there is always enough.
6. Remember it is the job of the singer to create new culture, not merely to regurgitate what exists.
7. When someone offers advice, smile and nod graciously. And listen.
8. "Have no fear of perfection – you'll never reach it." – Salvador Dali.
9. Your family is biased. Whether positive or negative, their views are skewed and are not an accurate reflection of your work in the world.
10. Accepting things in your life is not the same as agreeing. Learning to accept is a pathway to peace and wisdom.